Davina's
5 WEEKS TO
SUGAR-FREE

Davina's
5 WEEKS TO
SUGAR-FREE

Davina McCall

To Caroline and Milly...
Thank you for being the best sisters xxx

First published in Great Britain in 2015
by Orion Publishing Group Ltd
Orion House, 5 Upper St Martin's Lane
London WC2H 9EA
An Hachette UK Company

10 9 8 7 6 5 4 3 2 1

A CIP catalogue record for this book is available from
the British Library.

ISBN: 978 1 4091 5765 6

Designer: Paul Palmer-Edwards, Grade Design
Photographer: Andrew Hayes-Watkins
Art direction: Helen Ewing, Loulou Clark
Food director: Catherine Phipps
Food stylists: Anna Burges-Lumsden, Kate Blinman
Props stylists: Linda Berlin, Rebecca Newport, Loulou Clark
Project editor: Jinny Johnson
Proofreader: Elise See Tai
Indexer: Vicki Robinson

Nutritional analysis calculated by: Fiona Hunter, Bsc (Hons)
Nutrition, Dip Dietetics

Davina's nutritionist: Max Tomlinson ND
www.maxhealth.uk.com

Printed and bound in Germany

*Note: While every effort has been made to ensure that the
information in this book is correct, it should not be substituted
for medical advice. The recipes in this book should be used in
combination with a healthy lifestyle. If you are concerned
about any aspect of your health, speak to your GP. People
under medical supervision should not come off their
medication without speaking to their health professional.*

The Orion Publishing Group's policy is to use papers that
are natural, renewable and recyclable products and made
from wood grown in sustainable forests. The logging and
manufacturing processes are expected to conform to the
environmental regulations of the country of origin.

www.orionbooks.co.uk

Contents

Hi, my name is Davina and I'm a sugar addict.

How do I know? Because:

- I used to have three teaspoons of sugar in my tea and coffee.

- I used to eat five bags (at least!!!) of Haribos on a Friday night when filming *Big Brother*.

- I've stolen chocolate from my children's secret stashes and not told them.

- I've even scoffed chocolate last thing at night, just before cleaning my teeth.

Whenever I'd had a sugar pig out, I felt rubbish; so angry and disappointed with myself. I'd have huge slumps in energy, I gained weight and my clothes felt uncomfortable. Even my skin felt prickly – I hated it. Then I started reading about all the health benefits of cutting back on sugar, and not just for me – for my family too! Could we do it?

Let's get one thing straight right from the beginning: I LOVE my food. I'm half French – need I say more?

I love cooking and eating nice family grub and I want to enjoy every moment of it. I also want to eat well and healthily, and feed my family food that they like and does them good. But I don't want to become obsessive about it and be so busy weighing out sunflower seeds that all the fun goes out of mealtimes.

I'm a busy woman, working and looking after my kids, and I have to admit, I do glaze over a bit when I try to take in all the conflicting dietary advice that seems to fill the media. Eat carbs or cut carbs? Should I be eating low-fat or not? Cut out wheat? Stop dairy? OMG – what do I do? I just want a sensible, healthy way of eating, with the minimum of fuss.

We've all got so much to do. How do we figure out what we should be eating and then find the time to cook it?

One minute I'm doing an online shop on the way to work, then cooking meals for children, then another one for me and my husband – if juggling was an Olympic sport I'd win Gold!

Sometimes I feel intimidated by the glowing super-healthy gurus telling me what I should and shouldn't be putting in my mouth. I'm sure they're brilliant, but they do make me feel a little bit rubbish about myself.

So what to do? I'm no expert . . . but I've found people who are and I've got a plan. A plan that's worked for me and could work for you too.

I've talked to dieticians and a wonderful cook and we've come up with a way of eating that suits me and my family, cuts back on sugar and keeps us trim and in tip-top health.

We've put together a collection of recipes and a 5 week meal plan that I'm so excited about. These recipes have transformed my eating habits and helped me to lose weight and ditch my sweet tooth. I want to wean my kids off the white stuff too (as much as I can – completely seems almost impossible and unrealistic), so the recipes are family friendly. A treat for the children every now and again is great, but with so many health concerns surrounding sugar, I want them to lose that taste for sweetness.

What I love, love, love about these recipes:

- They're simple and delicious!

- No long lists of ingredients – who's got time for that?

- The ingredients are available in all good supermarkets.

Now here's the thing: *cutting back on sugar means cutting out processed foods.* If you buy and cook food that's had as little done to it as possible, you'll eat well and live well.

- -

MY SIMPLE RULES TO HEALTHY EATING:

- Cut out added sugar. Use only honey and maple syrup and work towards cutting those out as much as possible if you can. When buying maple syrup, check the label and make sure you get the real thing and avoid anything called 'maple-flavoured syrup' which will be mostly corn syrup.

- Cut out white rice, white flour, white pasta and white bread. Instead go for brown rice or barley, wholewheat or spelt pasta, bread and flour. And don't worry – there's nothing scary about spelt. It's just another sort of grain and you can buy it everywhere now.

- Don't eat ready meals and processed foods such as ready-made sauces. Yes, they are convenient, but many are packed full of sugar to make them taste better.

- Eat plenty of fresh vegetables and fruit. All these recipes contain loads.

- Watch out for low-fat foods such as fruit yoghurts, which may be laden with sugar. Buy full-fat plain yoghurt instead.

- Use butter not margarine, and whole milk, not skimmed.

- Drink plenty of water – still or sparkling. Flavour your water with slices of lemon or orange, cucumber, or herbs such as mint or lemongrass for variety.

- Use herbs and spices for flavouring your food and making it extra delicious.

- Eat foods as close to their natural state as possible. No processed gubbins.

Why is sugar so bad?

For years, some scientists have been trying to tell us that it's sugar – not fats – that's the big bugbear in our diets. It upsets our blood sugar and insulin levels and encourages fat storage and many believe that sugar is contributing to the rise and rise in obesity, and of type 2 diabetes and other ailments. Some of the converts to a no-sugar diet have even said that they have fewer wrinkles and spots since giving it up – WOW! Sugar is a problem now because we're all eating way too much. *We don't need it!*

This is really something we can work on. I can help myself look and feel better and improve my kids' health by making some simple changes in my way of eating.

Is sugar addictive?

I know it is for me. The more sweet things I have, the more I want. After Christmas, when the house has been full of chocolates, cakes and other sweet treats, I really crave sweetness and it takes a few weeks to get back to normal.

Sugar gives you a quick high. We all know that feeling when you're really tired and hungry and you think only a chocolate bar will do. It does do the trick – briefly. But then you crash and feel worse than before, so you want more and more sugar to help pick yourself up again.

Naughty 'hidden' sugar piles on the weight and makes you feel rubbish

I've certainly been guilty of eating too much sugar. The trouble is that it's not as simple as just giving up sugar in your coffee or that lunchtime chocolate bar. The big problem is the hidden sugar in foods.

Did you know that it's almost impossible to find any shop-bought mayo that doesn't contain sugar? I didn't realise that ketchup, canned soups and sauces, and ready meals are all laden with the stuff. Some of the worst offenders are the low-fat foods such as fruity yoghurts, which can contain five teaspoons of sugar. Even a glass of fruit juice or one of those healthy-looking smoothies contains as much sugar as a fizzy drink – far better to eat the fruit itself.

I've stopped buying table sugar – brown and white – and instead I keep some honey and maple syrup in my kitchen. At least they're closer to their natural state and they contain some nutrients. I've also cleared out the other stuff – pickles, canned soup, and so on. I'm trying to chuck out my ketchup – I really am – but I know this is a process. By cutting out sugar, you automatically stop eating so many of the things that just don't do you much good and make you pile on the pounds. It's simple.

So why all the savoury stuff?

I can hear you asking where the sugar is in asparagus and roast chicken? Why this book has more savoury recipes than sweet? I can explain. It's because the sugar in our system doesn't just come from bars of chocolate and sweet cakes. It comes from food that releases energy quickly, and this includes processed refined carbs, such as white flour, rice and pasta. These foods cause our blood sugar to rise and give us a quick boost – but that boost doesn't last, and eventually these highs and lows cause damage to our systems. Foods that contain lots

WHAT ABOUT . . .

Fruit?

This is one of the questions I asked because fruit is sweet, it contains fructose (fruit sugar). However, fruit also contains fibre, which balances out the fructose and makes it healthier for our bodies. Think about it – you can easily swallow a glass of fruit juice that may contain the juice of half a dozen apples, so loads of fructose, but eating more than a couple of apples is a real struggle.

Fruit is nature's package – it's the way we're meant to eat fructose. The fibre in fruit offsets the sugar and makes it less likely to cause energy spikes.

Dairy?

It turns out that it's better to have whole milk and yoghurt and forget the low-fat stuff. Milk is not that high in fat anyway and the low-fat versions are less nutritious, as they contain lower levels of fat-soluble vitamins such as A and E.

Alcohol?

I don't drink but my friends do. I don't remember the taste of booze, but I do know it's full of sugar and contains empty calories.

While you're on the 5 week plan, try to cut out the alcohol. You'll see a drop in weight and you'll feel better.

Here are the booze facts: red wine is better than white, as it contains less sugar. Spirits such as gin and vodka are OK, but beware of the mixers – tonic water has loads of sugar. Go with soda water or on the rocks. Beer is better than cider. Remember, though, that alcohol is high in calories and those are empty calories – they're not doing you any good. Make sure you have a few alcohol-free days every week to give your liver a rest.

If you are a non-drinker, try cutting out fizzy drinks, even diet ones, for 5 weeks, and see what happens. I have the occasional diet drink as a treat if I'm out.

AND WHAT ABOUT CALORIE COUNTING?

OMG, I've tried every diet going and I am so over the whole calorie-counting thing, which left me SO hungry. Instead I now focus on swapping nutrient-light junk foods, which are full of empty calories and do you no good, for nutrient-dense foods which are packed with goodness. Sounds complicated but it's really not. If you want to look and feel your best, you just have to feed your body the right things and make good choices. Here are some examples to explain what I mean.

Nasty nutrient-light foods

✘ White bread

✘ Chocolate bar

✘ Ice cream

✘ Sugary breakfast cereal

Good nutrient-dense foods

✔ Proper wholemeal spelt bread

✔ Raw veg sticks and hummus

✔ Plain yoghurt and fresh berries

✔ Oat porridge with a dash of maple syrup

of fibre, such as green vegetables, release energy more slowly and that is better for our bodies and our digestion. So my plan is to cut out the junk and think fresh foods – wholegrain bread, brown rice, plenty of vegetables, unprocessed meat, whole fruit not juice. Better for you, better for your family, better for your life – and you'll never be hungry!

The sugar challenge

As you all know, I'm always up for a challenge and this has been my biggest yet: I decided to wean myself and my family off sugar!

At first the idea of giving up processed foods and cutting sugar down, then out, seemed like a very major challenge, if I'm honest, but not impossible. So armed with everything I'd learned I made a start. First to go was the obvious stuff – the added table sugar, the bought cakes, the biscuits, the chocolate bars. Then went the processed food, such as white rice and white bread, as well as jars of sauces and ready meals.

With the help of my team, I looked at the things that I love to make for my family and myself and we adapted them to a healthier lifestyle. We took out the bad stuff – white flour, white rice, table sugar, all the junk – and came up with the most amazing recipes that I know you're going to love.

Now I'm making good simple meals from scratch, using non-processed, unrefined ingredients as far as possible. That means ignoring most of the processed packaged foods in the supermarket and filling my basket with fresh veg and fruit, eggs, meat, fish and fibre-rich wholegrains.

I leave the skins on regular white potatoes for the extra fibre, and I make pastry for my chicken pot pie with wholewheat spelt flour, instead of white flour. We eat loads of delicious chicken, meat and fish, and all kinds of salads packed with lovely fresh veg. We make mini-pizzas with wholewheat pitta and yummy things on multigrain toast. We feast on omelettes and frittatas and super soups.

We even make a few puds and cakes, replacing table sugar with honey or maple syrup. And yes, I know these are forms of sugar too, but we use as little as possible and this is real life after all. I'm not perfect.

And you know what? The sugar challenge is not that difficult after all.

You don't need fancy, weird, expensive stuff. You don't need to mix up strange green concoctions in your blender. With just a few adjustments you can cook healthier versions of family food and do everyone a power of good.

THE SCARY SCIENCE BIT

Don't just take my word for it. Many experts are saying that too much sugar is ruining our health, providing too many empty calories and contributing to rising obesity. Our bodies can't cope with this sugary overload and rates of type 2 diabetes are soaring.

Back in 2002 the World Health Organisation (WHO) said that everyone should cut back their sugar intake to 10 per cent or less of total daily calories. So for someone consuming 2,000 calories a day that is 50 grams of sugar. Some popular chocolate bars contain almost as much as that and one can of fizzy drink may contain 39 grams of sugar. Even a serving of canned soup may have as much as 10 grams of sugar.

The latest advice from the Scientific Advisory Committee on Nutrition in Britain goes even further and suggests cutting your intake of free sugars to 25 grams (5–6 teaspoons) a day for women and 35 grams (7–8 teaspoons) for men. 'Free' sugar is any sugar added to foods by manufacturers, cooks and consumers, plus the sugar naturally present in honey, syrups and fruit juices. It does not include the sugars in milk, dairy foods, vegetables and whole fruit.

The SACN report also recommends increasing the amount of fibre-rich food in our diet – whole grains, veg and fruit. And that's the advice I'm following in the recipes in this book.

More research needs to be done on the effects of sugar on our bodies, but for me cutting it out as much as possible makes nothing but sense. Sugary foods are empty calories after all. They don't do you any good so you're much better off without them.

HIDDEN SUGAR

Once you've started on my eating plan you'll be buying fewer packaged foods anyway, but do keep checking labels on any products you do choose, as you'll be surprised to discover where hidden sugar lurks. Here are some of the many different names for sugar to watch out for:

- Barley malt syrup
- Beet sugar
- Brown rice syrup
- Cane juice crystals
- Corn sweetener
- Corn syrup
- Dextrin
- Dextrose
- Fructose
- Fruit juice concentrate
- Glucose
- Invert sugar
- Lactose
- Malt syrup
- Maltodextrin
- Maltose
- Palm sugar
- Rice syrup
- Saccharose
- Sucrose
- Xlyose

. . . and there are many more.

The good news is that these recipes are quick and easy to make and so yummy you really won't feel deprived or hungry – I promise. This is not a weight-loss diet as such, but it will keep you trim because you won't be taking in empty calories in the form of sweeties and processed foods.

All my recipes can be made from ingredients found in most supermarkets. You don't have to order stuff from special websites. I do, though, have lots more spices and herbs in my cupboard now than I used to and they're great for adding that extra zip and flavour to food. One of the reasons food manufacturers add sugar to their products is to make them taste nice, to appeal to the sweet tooth they've taught us to have. I've learned to add flavour with herbs and spices and it's a much better idea.

What's in my book

- Easy recipes for fabulous family meals, including roasts, pies, risottos, soups and salads.

- Most recipes have fewer than 12 or so main ingredients (not counting salt and pepper), all of which are available in supermarkets.

- No complicated cooking techniques so the recipes don't take too long to make.

- We've cut out the bad stuff so you don't have to think about it. Just follow the recipes.

- No refined white sugar in anything, but there are some sweet treats, made with honey and maple syrup, if you want. That's up to you. When I'm going cold turkey I do without them.

- A 5 week eating plan to curb that sweet tooth.

How to use this book

Short sharp shock or the gentle option?
As far as added sugar goes you can cut it right out, today. It might be hard at first – you'll miss sugar, even crave it, but you can do it. And it will get easier. The less sugar you eat, the less you'll find you want.

Or you can do what I did and take the gentler option. Follow the recipes in this book, including the occasional sweet treat made with maple syrup and honey. Over a period of five weeks, reduce the sweet stuff until you're not having any at all. That's right! You've kicked the sugar habit and it really wasn't that hard. To do it this way, follow my 5 week plan on pages 216–218. You'll be eating so well you won't miss the other stuff, believe me.

I love every one of these recipes and so do my family and friends. I hope you enjoy them as much as I do! Love, Davina xx

Davina's favourites

1 Breakfast & Brunch

"Super healthy – but sometimes a little bit naughty. That's my sort of breakfast."

American-style fluffy pancakes

Traditional American pancakes are made with buttermilk, which gives them that lovely fluffiness. But I've discovered that if, like me, you don't always have buttermilk in the fridge, you can get the same effect by souring ordinary milk with a dash of lemon. It thickens the milk and the pancakes work a treat. Keep the pancakes warm in a low oven while you make a stack, then serve them with bacon and maple syrup for a USA vibe, or with blueberries and crème fraiche to stay sugar-free.

1 Turn the oven on and set it very low – about 140°C/120°C Fan/Gas 1 – to keep the pancakes warm as you make them.

2 Add the lemon juice to the milk and stir well. Leave the mixture to stand for 5 minutes or so until it has thickened – you've just made some buttermilk! This hint of sourness makes the pancakes lighter and fluffier.

3 Lightly beat the egg and add it to the buttermilk along with the vanilla seeds – just split the pod and scrape the seeds out into the mixture with your thumb.

4 Put the flour in a large bowl and whisk in the baking powder, bicarbonate of soda and cinnamon. Make a well in the middle and gradually stir in the buttermilk and egg mixture, making sure the batter is as lump free as possible.

5 Melt the butter or coconut oil in a large frying pan, then tip the melted fat into the batter and stir well. Wipe the inside of the frying pan with a piece of kitchen towel.

6 Place the frying pan on the heat and add a few blobs of the batter, keeping them well spaced; roughly 2 tablespoons per pancake should be about right. Cook the pancakes on one side until you can see the batter starting to set around the edges, then flip them over – the underside should have browned nicely. Cook the pancakes for another couple of minutes.

7 Keep the pancakes warm in the oven while you make the rest, then serve in a stack with blueberries and crème fraiche if you like.

Makes about 16

juice of ½ lemon
225ml whole milk
1 egg
½ vanilla pod
175g wholewheat spelt flour
1 tsp baking powder
¼ tsp bicarbonate of soda
pinch of cinnamon
1 tbsp soft butter or coconut oil
blueberries (optional)
crème fraiche (optional)

Crêpes

Lovely for breakfast or any time of day, these crêpes are so easy to make and very light. Serve them with a drizzle of maple syrup or honey or just with some wedges of orange to squeeze over. Or you could stay sugar-free and eat your crêpes with melted cheese or smoked salmon. The spelt flour works brilliantly so don't be scared of it. You use it just like ordinary flour but it's better for you.

1 Turn the oven on and set it very low – about 140°C/120°C Fan/ Gas 1 – to keep the crêpes warm as you make them.

2 Put the flour and salt in a large bowl and whisk briefly to remove any lumps. Make a well in the centre of the flour and add the egg. Start whisking the flour into the egg and gradually add the milk, a little at a time.

3 When everything is mixed in, leave the batter to stand for a while – this will allow the flour to absorb the milk.

4 When you are ready to make the crêpes, melt the butter in a non-stick frying pan, then pour it into the batter and stir. Wipe the pan over with a piece of kitchen towel.

5 Hold the frying pan in one hand and a small ladle in the other. Pour a ladleful of batter into the pan and swirl it around, then place the pan on the heat. As soon as the crêpe has set and started to brown around the edges, flip it over with a spatula and let it cook for another minute or so. Transfer the crêpe to a plate and keep it warm in the oven while you make the rest. Serve as soon as possible, with whatever accompaniments you want.

Makes 10—12

125g wholemeal spelt flour
pinch of salt
1 egg
300ml whole milk
1 tbsp soft butter
honey or maple syrup (optional)

Home-made granola

You won't believe how easy this granola is to make and it's so much cheaper than all the luxury versions in the shops. The egg white helps bind the mixture together beautifully without using lots of syrup, and the coconut oil has a great flavour with natural sweetness. You can add dried fruit but it does up the sugar content so try it without first.

1 Preheat the oven to 150°C/130°C Fan/Gas 2. Line a large baking tray with greaseproof paper.

2 Put the oats, coconut, nuts and salt in a large bowl. If your coconut oil has set, warm it gently in a pan until just melted. Pour the oil and the maple syrup over the dry ingredients and mix thoroughly so everything is well coated.

3 Whisk the egg white until it's frothy. Pour this over the oat mixture and mix thoroughly again. Spread the granola over the baking tray as evenly as you can.

4 Bake the granola in the oven for 40–50 minutes, turning it over half way through. Start checking after 40 minutes to see if it's done – it should be lightly browned and dry.

5 Remove the tray of granola from the oven and leave it to cool completely. Gently break up the granola into clumps as big or small as you want. You will find some of the mixture is loose, but that's unavoidable so don't worry.

6 Store the granola in an airtight jar – it will keep well for a few weeks. Enjoy it with milk or yoghurt, or just in handfuls when you feel like a yummy snack.

Makes 10–12 portions

250g jumbo oats

50g desiccated or flaked coconut

150g nuts, lightly crushed into pieces (any kind are good, but almonds add sweetness)

a pinch of salt

3 tbsp coconut oil (or another type of oil, but coconut oil is best)

2 tbsp maple syrup

1 egg white

Bircher muesli

I always used to roll my eyes when anyone suggested making muesli, but how wrong was I! This is so easy and quick and I can feel smug while eating it. I love smug. This amount feeds two, but just double up the ingredients if you want more. I dilute the juice to reduce the sugar and you could also try using coconut milk instead if you fancy.

1 Put the oats, wheatgerm and cinnamon in a bowl and pour over the apple juice and 125ml of water. Mix everything together well, then cover and leave in the fridge overnight.

2 In the morning, remove the cores from the apples but don't peel them. Grate the apples into the muesli, then stir in the yoghurt. Sprinkle with nuts or seeds and drizzle with honey or maple syrup if you like.

Serves 2

100g porridge oats
2 tbsp wheatgerm
large pinch of cinnamon
125ml apple juice
2 eating apples
100ml yoghurt
chopped nuts or seeds (optional)
honey or maple syrup (optional)

Proper porridge

I always loved the idea of proper porridge but used shortcuts such as packets and microwave methods so it never tasted that good. Actually, it's ridiculously simple to make so I don't know what I was worried about. The cinnamon is a great touch and let's rock the whole milk. Keeps the family full for ages.

1 Put the oats in a saucepan and pour over the milk or milk and water. Slowly bring the mixture to the boil, stirring constantly, then turn the heat down. Add the salt and cinnamon.

2 Cook the porridge gently, stirring regularly, until it has thickened to your liking. As long as the oats have cooked for about 5 minutes, you can eat it as runny or as thick as you like.

3 If you have a sweet tooth, serve with a little honey or maple syrup and gradually cut this down until you don't need it any more.

Serves 1

50g porridge oats
350ml whole milk or a
    combination of milk and water
pinch of salt
pinch of cinnamon
1 tsp maple syrup or honey
    (optional)

Multigrain seeded bread

Home-made bread is so the best, whether you make it by hand or in a machine. Most of the shop-bought stuff contains loads of sugar. Have a good look at the packet when you're buying the flour, as some of the malted versions are based on white flour. You want wholemeal.

1 Put the flour and seeds in a large bowl. Sprinkle the yeast into the flour, then give it a stir and add the salt – you don't want the salt and yeast landing directly on top of one another.

2 Add the malt extract to 300–350ml of warm water and stir until it is dissolved. Gradually add this to the flour, mixing until you have a dough. If the dough seems quite dry, add more water, but make sure you've mixed it thoroughly before you do this, as dough can be very wet inside and seem quite dry on the surface.

3 Turn the dough on to a lightly floured work surface and knead it thoroughly until smooth. Put the dough back in the bowl and cover it with cling film or a damp tea towel. Leave it somewhere warm for a couple of hours until it is well risen (about double the volume) and springy to touch.

4 Knock the dough back, then lightly knead it again and shape it into either a loaf to fit a greased 1kg loaf tin or leave it more free-form and place it on a greased baking tray. Cover again with cling film or a damp tea towel and leave it to rise.

5 When the dough has been rising for half an hour, preheat your oven to its highest setting. After another half an hour the bread should be ready to bake. Put the bread in the oven and turn the heat down to 220°C/200°C Fan/Gas 7. Bake the loaf for 30–35 minutes, until it's well risen and brown. The loaf should also sound hollow when tapped on the bottom.

6 Remove the loaf from the oven and leave it to cool on a rack before slicing and eating – if you can wait that long!

Makes 1 loaf

500g malted wholemeal flour, plus extra for dusting work surface
100g mixed seeds (sunflower, flax, sesame)
7g sachet of instant dried yeast
1 tsp salt
1 tbsp malt extract
butter or oil, for greasing loaf tin or baking tray

Poached eggs with avocado on toast

This is one of my very favourite things. For years I didn't do poached eggs because I couldn't understand the whole whirlpool thing, but now – you can't stop me. You need to stir frantically to make a swirling vortex of water, then drop your egg in very quickly. You'll think it's all going wrong but it isn't. Trust me – I'm a presenter. Use really fresh eggs, cold from the fridge, for best results. If they're cold the whites will be firmer.

1 Bring a saucepan of water to the boil, then turn the heat down slightly until the water is simmering. Break an egg into a small cup.

2 Swirl a spoon around in the water to make a whirlpool – really get the water going – then drop the egg in. Cook the egg for about 2½ minutes, until the white is set and the yolk is still runny, then remove the egg with a slotted spoon so the water drains away from it. Repeat with as many eggs as you want to cook.

3 Meanwhile, toast the bread and spread with butter. Cut the avocado in half and remove the stone, then mash the flesh with the lime juice and seasoning. Spread the mashed avocado on to the toast and top with the poached eggs when they're ready.

- -

Davina's tip
If you need to make lots of poached eggs, it's best not to try to cook them all at once in the same saucepan. Instead, cook each egg individually for just 2 minutes and set them all aside. When you have cooked them all, carefully drop them back into the water and cook for another 30 seconds. That way they will all be ready at the same time.

Serves 2

1–2 very fresh eggs per person
2 slices of wholemeal seeded
    bread
butter, for spreading
1 avocado
1 tsp lime juice
salt and black pepper

Pitted bagels

This is a huge favourite in our house and something my husband taught me how to do. You cut the bagels in half, then use your index finger to roll the doughy bit out of the middle. Then pop the bagels in the toaster briefly and you get a lovely crisp, hollow shell to fill with dollops of delicious stuff. I've suggested fillings here but I'm sure you'll think up plenty of others. And by the way – blitz the doughy bits to make breadcrumbs and stash them in the freezer so there's no waste.

1 Cut the bagels in half. Scoop out most of the inside of each bagel with your fingers or a teaspoon. You'll find that once you get hold of the dough, most of it will peel out very easily. Lightly toast the bagels.

2 For the egg mayonnaise filling, run the cooked eggs under cold water until they're cool enough to handle. Peel the eggs and put them in a bowl. Mash them with a fork, season with salt and pepper and stir in the mayonnaise and the Tabasco, if using. Pile the mixture into the pitted bagels.

3 For the cream cheese and smoked salmon filling, mix the cream cheese with the crème fraiche, then stir in the smoked salmon. Add a squeeze of lime juice and season with pepper. Pile the mixture into the bagels and garnish with dill or chives.

4 For the avocado, tomato and bacon filling, finely dice the bacon and fry it until crisp and brown. Mix with the avocado and tomato, season with salt and pepper, then pile the mixture into the bagels.

Davina's tip
Sometimes, when I'm in a real rush in the morning, I toast a pitted bagel and just sprinkle it with a dash of olive oil and some salt and black pepper – love it!

2 wholemeal bagels

Egg mayonnaise filling
4 eggs, hard-boiled for 7 minutes
2 tbsp Davina's mayonnaise
   (see page 210)
dash of Tabasco (optional)
salt and black pepper

Cream cheese and smoked salmon filling
150g cream cheese or Boursin
1 tbsp crème fraiche
100g smoked salmon, torn into
   small pieces
squeeze of lime
sprigs of dill or some finely
   chopped chives to garnish
black pepper

Avocado, tomato and bacon filling
4 rashers of smoked back bacon
1 large avocado, roughly mashed
1 tomato, finely diced
salt and black pepper

Bacon and mushroom omelette

Eggs are amazing. End of. And everything tastes better with bacon.

1 Heat the olive oil in a frying pan and add the onion and bacon. Fry them gently over a medium heat until the bacon is brown and crisp. Add the mushrooms and thyme, if using, and cook until the mushrooms are soft, stirring often.

2 Remove the onion, bacon and mushrooms from the frying pan and set them aside. Wipe the pan with kitchen towel, then set it over a low to medium heat and add the butter. When the butter is melted and foaming, season the eggs with salt and pepper and pour them into the frying pan.

3 Cook the omelette for a few moments until the underside has set, then use a fork to pull the sides into the middle until most of the omelette is set. Leave to cook for another a minute or so until it is done to your liking – some people like to keep the centre runny while others prefer it cooked through.

4 Sprinkle over the cheese, if using, then pile the bacon and mushroom filling over one half of the omelette. Flip the other half of the omelette over the filling, divide it in two and serve immediately.

Serves 2

1 tbsp olive oil
1 small onion, finely chopped
100g streaky bacon, chopped
200g mushrooms, wiped and sliced
a few small sprigs of thyme (optional)
1 tbsp butter
4 eggs, lightly beaten
50g Cheddar or Gruyère cheese, grated (optional)
salt and black pepper

Kedgeree

I love kedgeree and although I find it a bit too hearty for breakfast it makes a perfect brunch – or lunch. Or even supper! I'm not a fan of hot curries but I do like the mild curry spice in this. I use brown rice, of course. For an extra-speedy version you could buy some hot-smoked salmon and just flake it in at the end.

1 Rinse the rice well, then leave it to soak in cold water for 10 minutes.

2 Put the smoked haddock in a saucepan wide enough to hold it in one layer and cover with water. Bring it to the boil, then immediately turn off the heat, cover the pan and leave it to stand for 10 minutes.

3 After 10 minutes, strain off the cooking liquid into a large jug and, if necessary, add more water until you have 450ml of liquid. When the fish is cool enough to handle, break it into flakes, discarding any skin and bones, and set it aside.

4 Heat the butter in a large saucepan or casserole dish. Add the onion and cook it very slowly until it's soft and translucent, then add the curry powder. Drain the rice and add it to the pan, then pour in the reserved cooking liquid. Season with pepper, but not with salt, as the haddock will have made the cooking liquid quite salty.

5 Bring to the boil, then turn the heat right down and cover the pan. Leave the rice to cook for 25 minutes, then remove the pan from the heat. Add the peas, then cover the pan again and leave to steam for at least another 5 minutes, off the heat, so all the liquid is absorbed into the rice.

6 Fluff up the rice with a fork and gently stir in the smoked haddock. Leave the kedgeree to stand for another couple of minutes to let the fish warm through. Serve garnished with the quartered eggs and a sprinkling of coriander leaves if you like.

Serves 4

200g brown rice
300g smoked haddock fillet, preferably undyed
a small knob of butter
1 onion, finely chopped
2 tsp mild curry powder (see Davina's spice blend, page 213)
150g peas (frozen are fine)
4 eggs, hard-boiled and quartered
chopped fresh coriander (optional)
black pepper

Frittatas

Have I mentioned that I think eggs are amazing? Well let me tell you again – they are. My husband doesn't like eggs that much, but I can get him to eat these frittatas because they are really loaded with veg and other good stuff and have just a hint of egg.

Mediterranean frittata

1 Preheat the oven to 200°C/180°C Fan/Gas 6.

2 Spread the onions, courgette and red peppers in a roasting tin. Drizzle them with a tablespoon of olive oil and mix well so all the vegetables are lightly coated. Season them with salt and black pepper and sprinkle with the oregano. Place the roasting tin in the oven and roast the vegetables for 30 minutes, then remove them from the oven and set aside.

3 Beat the eggs in a bowl with a fork and season with salt and pepper.

4 Add a teaspoon of olive oil and a knob of butter to a large frying pan and heat until the butter has melted. Turn up the heat and quickly fry the mushrooms until they're lightly browned. Add the roast vegetables, spacing them out evenly across the frying pan. Then add the cherry tomatoes and sprinkle a few leaves of basil on top. Preheat the grill to its highest setting.

5 Pour the eggs into the pan with the vegetables and cook until the base is well browned and starting to set around the edges.

6 Put the frying pan with the frittata under the preheated grill for a couple of minutes until it is set, puffed up and starting to turn a lovely light golden brown. Remove the frittata from the grill and cut it into wedges to serve.

Serves 4

2 red onions, peeled and cut into wedges
1 courgette, cut into rounds
2 red peppers, sliced lengthways
olive oil
1 tsp dried oregano
6 eggs
knob of butter
200g mushrooms, wiped and cut into quarters
6 cherry tomatoes, halved
a handful of fresh basil leaves, torn
salt and black pepper

Chorizo frittata

1 Add the chorizo to a dry frying pan and cook until brown on both sides and much of the fat has come out. Using a slotted spoon, remove the chorizo from the pan and leave it to drain on some kitchen towel.

2 Pour off most of the chorizo fat from the frying pan and add the butter. When it has melted, add the onion and fry gently for 5 minutes until it's starting to turn translucent.

3 Then turn up the heat and add the potatoes to the pan and fry them for another 4–5 minutes until the onions and potatoes have started to brown. Turn down the heat. Preheat the grill to its highest setting.

4 Add the spinach or rocket to the frying pan and let it wilt down for a couple of minutes, then add the thyme. Beat the eggs in a bowl.

5 Sprinkle the chorizo rounds over the spinach or rocket and potatoes, then pour in the eggs and make sure everything is evenly distributed over the pan. You probably won't need seasoning because of the spicy chorizo. Cook for about 5 minutes, until the base is well browned and starting to set around the edges.

6 Put the pan with the frittata under the preheated grill for a couple of minutes until it is set, puffed up and starting to turn light golden brown. Remove the frittata from the grill, cut it into wedges and serve.

Serves 4

100g cooking chorizo, sliced
   into thin rounds
a small knob of butter
1 onion, chopped
150g new potatoes, unpeeled,
   cooked and sliced into
   thick rounds
100g spinach or rocket leaves
a few sprigs of thyme
6 eggs

Pea, asparagus and broad bean frittata

1 Bring a small pan of water to the boil, add the asparagus tips and boil them for 2 minutes. Remove the asparagus with a slotted spoon and set aside. Bring the water back to the boil, add the beans and peas, then boil for 2 minutes. Drain them thoroughly and set aside.

2 Heat the olive oil in a large frying pan, then add the butter. When the butter has melted, add the spring onions and cook them for 2 minutes. Add the asparagus tips and cook for another few minutes until everything is starting to brown around the edges. Add the beans and peas to the pan.

3 Preheat the grill to its highest setting. Beat the eggs in a bowl and season with salt and pepper. Sprinkle the mint and the lemon zest, if using, into the pan, then pour in the eggs. Dot heaped teaspoons of the ricotta all over the top of the frittata.

4 Cook for about 5 minutes until the underside is cooked through. Put the pan with the frittata under the preheated grill for a couple of minutes until it is set, puffed up and starting to turn a light golden brown. Remove the frittata from the grill, cut into wedges and serve.

Serves 4

100g asparagus tips
100g broad beans (fresh or
   frozen)
100g peas (fresh or frozen)
1 tbsp olive oil
small knob of butter
2 spring onions, cut into rounds
6 eggs
½ tsp dried mint
1 tsp finely grated lemon zest
   (optional)
100g ricotta
salt and black pepper

Hash browns

OMG, my kids love this, with some poached or fried eggs. Keep the peel on the potatoes for extra fibre and dice them really small. When you're frying the potatoes, press them down well to make a neat cake, but if it all breaks when you try to turn it, don't worry. It still tastes just as good.

1 Put the potatoes in a saucepan, pour in enough water just to cover them and add half a teaspoon of salt. Using only just enough water helps to concentrate the starch which will help to hold the potatoes together later, when you're frying them. Bring the water to the boil and cook the potatoes for 3 minutes. Remove the pan from the heat and drain the potatoes in a colander.

2 Heat half the olive oil and butter in a frying pan. Add the onion and fry gently for 5 minutes until it's starting to brown a little around the edges. Add the potatoes and season them with salt and pepper. Stir to mix the onions and potatoes together, then use a spatula to press everything down into a single layer. Keeping the heat low to medium, cook for 10–15 minutes until the underside is well browned.

3 Take the pan off the heat, place a large plate over it and turn the pan to flip the potato cake on to the plate.

4 Heat the rest of the oil and butter in the frying pan. Slide the potato cake back into the frying pan – brown side uppermost – and cook for a further 10 minutes to brown the underside. Serve cut into wedges and serve with eggs or whatever you fancy.

Serves 4

500g potatoes (Maris Pipers or King Edwards are both good), unpeeled and cut into 1cm dice
2 tbsp olive oil
2 tbsp butter
1 onion, finely chopped
salt and black pepper

Davina's favourites

2 Starters & Small Plates

"Yummy treats to enjoy as starters, light lunches or whenever you like. None of your processed rubbish."

Figs with prosciutto and goat's cheese

This is a starter staple in our house and everyone absolutely loves it. It's so easy and really quick to make. I like goat's cheese but you can use any softish cheese you like.

1 Preheat the oven to 220°C/200°C Fan/Gas 7.

2 Cut the tips off the figs and slice a deep cross in each, almost to the base. Squeeze the figs from the bottom, so the points of the quarters splay outwards a little. Put about a dessertspoon of cheese in the centre of each fig.

3 Wrap each fig in 2 slices of the prosciutto, leaving the tops exposed. Place the wrapped figs in a roasting dish and put them in the preheated oven for about 10 minutes, until the ham is crisp and the cheese has started to melt.

4 To make the dressing, whisk the oil and vinegar together and season with salt and black pepper.

5 Put handfuls of rocket leaves on individual plates. Place a fig in the centre of each pile and drizzle the dressing on top.

Serves 4 as a starter (or double up to feed more)

4 figs
small tub of soft goat's cheese (or similar), about 125g
8 slices of prosciutto
bag of rocket leaves

Dressing
2 tbsp olive oil
2 tsp balsamic vinegar
salt and black pepper

Asparagus mimosa

OK, I know there was never any sugar in this classic dish, but I love it and it takes me back to my childhood in France so I had to have it in my book. It's finely chopped hard-boiled egg sprinkled over asparagus, but you can make it with other vegetables, such as French beans, if you like.

1 Bring a saucepan of water to the boil and add the eggs. Simmer them for 8 minutes, then drain and plunge them in a bowl of cold water to stop the cooking.

2 When the eggs are cool enough to handle, remove the shells. Separate the egg whites from the yolks and grate or finely chop them into separate bowls.

3 Bend each asparagus spear, with more emphasis on the bottom of the stem, until it snaps – this will give you just the tender, non-woody part of the stem. Wash the asparagus thoroughly in cold water and discard the woody ends.

4 Bring another pan of water to the boil, add the asparagus spears and cook them for 3 minutes until just tender. Drain them thoroughly and arrange on 4 plates.

5 To make the dressing, whisk the olive oil and mustard with the lemon juice in a small jug. Season the dressing with salt and pepper, then drizzle it over the asparagus.

6 Sprinkle the chopped egg whites, then the yolks over the asparagus and serve.

Serves 4 as a starter

2 eggs
2 bunches of asparagus

Dressing
1 tbsp olive oil
¼ tsp Dijon mustard
juice of ½ lemon
salt and black pepper

Brown shrimp and spinach tartlets

Maybe you think you can't make pastry and you're not sure about spelt flour. Give it a go and you'll be surprised – it's really not difficult and using spelt flour is no different to using ordinary flour. Brown shrimp are available in supermarkets or you can use potted shrimp instead – just remove the buttery layer on the top. And you'll notice I mention 'baking beans' in this recipe. These are just to keep the pastry flat when you're baking it without a filling. You can buy special ceramic baking beans but ordinary dried beans work just fine. You'll also need four 12cm tartlet tins.

1 To make the pastry, put the flour with a pinch of salt in a food processor or a bowl. Add the cubes of cold butter and either blitz or rub it in with your fingertips until the mixture is the consistency of fine breadcrumbs.

2 Add the egg yolk and 1 tablespoon of water and mix to form a dough. If the dough is too crumbly, add a little more water. Wrap the dough in cling film and chill for at least an hour. If you're in a hurry, you can chill the dough in the freezer for 10–15 minutes.

3 Preheat the oven to 200°C/180°C Fan/Gas 6. Divide the pastry into 4 balls and roll them out into rounds slightly larger than your tartlet tins. Line the tins with the pastry. Pierce the base of each all over with a fork, then line with baking parchment and add some baking beans.

4 Bake the pastry cases in the preheated oven for 15 minutes, then remove the beans and paper and bake for a further 10 minutes until the pastry is cooked through and light brown in colour. When the pastry is cool, trim the edges if necessary.

5 To make the filling, cut off any long stalks from the spinach. Bring a large pan of water to the boil, add the spinach and cook it briefly until wilted. Drain and press out as much water from the spinach as you can. Divide the spinach between the tartlet shells, then sprinkle over the lemon zest. Mix the brown shrimp with the lemon juice, then divide them between the tartlet shells. Season with salt and pepper.

6 Beat the eggs together, then add the double cream, season with salt and pepper and mix. Pour an equal amount of mixture into each tartlet over the spinach and shrimp, then finish with some grated nutmeg.

7 Bake the tartlets in the oven for 10–15 minutes until the egg mixture is set, with just a very slight wobble in the middle. Serve hot or cold.

Serves 4 as a starter

200g fresh spinach
1 tsp finely grated lemon zest
100g brown shrimp
1 tbsp lemon juice
2 eggs
150ml double cream
grated nutmeg
salt and black pepper

Pastry
200g wholemeal spelt flour
pinch of salt
110g cold butter, cubed
1 egg yolk
1–2 tbsp cold water

Prawn cocktail in avocado boats

A deliciously retro starter. I like to use the little prawns but go as prawny as you like and choose big ones if you prefer. Make your own mayo and ketchup to stay sugar-free.

1 First make the Marie Rose sauce by mixing the ingredients together in a small bowl. Season with salt and pepper, then taste and add more of any of the ingredients if necessary.

2 Peel the avocados and cut them in half. Slice a very thin piece away from the base of each avocado half to help it stand properly on the plate without toppling over. Rub the avocados all over with the cut lemon to stop them going brown, then season with salt and pepper.

3 Mix the prawns with the Marie Rose sauce, then divide them between the avocado pits. Serve with lemon wedges and a sprinkle of cayenne or paprika.

Serves 4 as a starter

2 ripe avocados
½ a lemon, plus lemon wedges
  for serving
250g peeled cooked prawns
cayenne or paprika, for serving
salt and black pepper

Marie Rose sauce
3 tbsp Davina's mayonnaise
  (see page 210)
1–2 tsp Davina's ketchup
  (see page 212)
dash of Tabasco
squeeze of lemon juice

Salmon tartare

I know, this is raw salmon but the amazing thing is that it gets 'cooked' in the dressing. Dice the fish really small and you can taste the goodness. Limes vary in sourness through the year so if your fruit is really tart you could just use the juice of half the lime with a tablespoon of orange juice. This is quick to prepare but needs to be chilled for half an hour before serving. Don't try to make it any further ahead or it will be too 'cooked'.

1 Put the salmon fillets in the freezer while you prepare the rest of the ingredients. This will firm them up and make dicing them much easier.

2 Put the cucumber, spring onions, coriander, mint and dill in a bowl. Mix the dressing ingredients in a small jug and season with salt and black pepper.

3 Remove a salmon fillet from the freezer. Cut it into thin strips, then dice – the dice should be about ½ centimetre square. Remove the remaining salmon fillet from the freezer and cut and dice it in the same way.

4 Add all the diced salmon to the bowl with the cucumber, spring onions and herbs and stir gently to combine. Season again with salt and black pepper.

5 Pour over the dressing and stir gently again to make sure all the salmon is coated. Chill in the fridge for half an hour. Serve the salmon on lettuce or endive leaves or crispbreads, and sprinkle with herbs and sesame seeds.

Serves 4

2 x 150g salmon fillets, skinned
¼ cucumber, deseeded and finely
  diced
2 spring onions, finely chopped
a few sprigs of coriander, mint
  and dill
little gem lettuce or endive
  leaves, or crispbreads
sprigs of fresh herbs, to garnish
black sesame seeds
salt and black pepper

Dressing
juice of 1 lime
1 tsp lime zest
1 tsp finely grated fresh root ginger
1 tbsp vegetable oil
½ tsp sesame oil

Roast tomato soup with mozzarella balls

We grow our own tomatoes and it's like 'The Day of the Triffids' in our greenhouse come summer. I take goody bags every time I go to see a friend. I had to have a recipe to use some of the tomatoes up and this one is a corker. It's great with or without the mozzarella balls but they do look very pretty for a party.

1 Preheat the oven to 200°C/180°C Fan/Gas 6.

2 Put the tomatoes, cut-side up, on a large baking tray or roasting dish. Tuck the unpeeled cloves of garlic in among them, then season with salt and pepper. Drizzle with 2 tablespoons of the olive oil and sprinkle over the dried herbs. Put the tray in the oven and roast the tomatoes for 40 minutes until they have softened and started to brown.

3 Meanwhile, heat the remaining olive oil in a saucepan. Add the onion, celery and carrot and cook over a very gentle heat for about 10 minutes until softened. Add the stock and simmer for about 5 minutes, then remove the pan from the heat and allow to cool.

4 Remove the tomatoes and garlic from the oven. As soon as the garlic cloves are cool enough to handle, squeeze out the flesh into a bowl and discard the skins. Put the tomatoes and garlic, along with any cooking juices left in the tray, into a blender and add the stock and vegetables. Blitz until smooth. Push the soup through a sieve back into the pan to catch any unblended tomato seeds.

5 Gently reheat the soup and serve with mozzarella ball floats, if using, and a few sprinkled basil leaves. You could also drizzle a little extra olive oil over the soup before serving.

Serves 4

1kg ripe tomatoes, cut in half
1 head of garlic, cloves separated but unpeeled
3 tbsp olive oil
1 tsp dried oregano or mixed dried herbs
1 large onion, finely chopped
1 celery stick, finely chopped
1 carrot, finely diced
600ml chicken or vegetable stock
salt and black pepper

To serve
150g small mozzarella balls (optional)
a handful of basil leaves
olive oil (optional)

French onion soup

This is a nod to my French heritage and it's a soup my kids love. It needs a stock with a really good flavour and the wine adds richness too – although you can leave it out if you prefer. Make sure you get the onions lovely and brown to give the soup a good colour.

1 Heat the olive oil and butter in a large saucepan, then add the onions and turn the heat down to low. Cover the saucepan and leave the onions to cook for 15–20 minutes, until soft. Stir every so often, just to make sure they aren't catching on the bottom of the pan.

2 Turn up the heat and continue to cook the onions, stirring regularly, until they've turned a deep golden brown. You will find that any liquid will evaporate during this process.

3 Add the thyme and garlic and stir for a couple of minutes and then pour in the wine or cider, if using. Allow it to bubble for a few minutes until it has almost completely evaporated. Add the stock and season with salt and black pepper, then simmer the soup for 20–25 minutes.

4 Preheat the grill to its highest setting. Toast the bread lightly on both sides, then divide the cheese between the slices of toast and press it down. Put the slices under the grill until the cheese has melted and is bubbling, and the bread has browned around the sides.

5 Put the toasted bread and cheese in deep bowls and ladle the soup on top. Serve piping hot.

Serves 4

1 tbsp olive oil
25g butter
1kg large, sweet onions, sliced
   into crescents
a large sprig of thyme
2 garlic cloves, finely chopped
250ml white wine or dry cider
   (optional)
1.2 litres well-flavoured chicken
   or beef stock
100g Gruyère cheese or similar,
   grated
4 thick slices of wholemeal
   sourdough bread
salt and black pepper

Davina's favourites

3 Big Soups & Salads

"I love, love, love this sort of food and could make these dishes every day.

PS: the key to a good soup is a good stock and loads of lovely veg."

Chicken noodle soup

My kids' favourite, this soup really is food for the soul. And I know that when my children grow up they will cook chicken noodle soup and it will be their kids' favourite. The key is good chicken stock, which I promise you is so easy to make – see my recipe on page 210. I'm suggesting adding raw chicken here, but you can also use cooked chicken and just add it at the end to warm through. I also use wholemeal spaghetti instead of ordinary noodles, but if you prefer something different, go ahead.

1 Heat the butter in a large saucepan and add the leeks and carrots. Stir until they are completely coated with butter, then cook slowly for 6–7 minutes until they've started to soften around the edges.

2 Add the garlic, cook for another minute, then add the stock and season with salt and black pepper.

3 Bring the soup to the boil. Break the wholemeal spaghetti into pieces and drop them into the soup. Turn the heat down and simmer until the spaghetti is completely cooked through – it should be quite soft, rather than al dente – and the vegetables are tender.

4 Cut the chicken into thin strips and add them to the pan for the final 3–4 minutes of cooking. Check that the chicken is cooked through and no pinkness remains. If you're using cooked chicken, add it for the last minute just to warm through.

5 Sprinkle with parsley before serving.

Serves 4–6

25g butter
3 leeks, sliced into rounds
2 carrots, diced
2 garlic cloves, crushed
1.3 litres well-flavoured chicken
    stock (see page 210)
50g wholemeal spaghetti
2 chicken breasts (or some
    cooked chicken)
handful of parsley, finely
    chopped
salt and black pepper

Chicken and vegetable soup

I love a chicken soup and this can be made with some leftover cooked chicken, plus any bits of stuffing or sausage meat if you have them. Vary the veg as you like – I sometimes use sweet potatoes instead of ordinary ones and they're delish!

1 Heat the olive oil in a large saucepan. Add the bacon and fry until it's crisp and brown, then add all the vegetables except the cabbage. Stir the vegetables for a minute or so over a high heat, then pour in the stock and season with salt and pepper. Bring the soup to the boil, then simmer for 20 minutes.

2 Add the cabbage and cook for another 15 minutes. You should find that the potatoes have broken down slightly and thickened the soup.

3 Finally, add the cooked chicken and warm it through. Serve the soup piping hot.

- -

Davina's tip
I never waste a chicken carcass! After the Sunday roast, I strip off all the remaining meat to have in a salad, then make a beautiful stock with the bones.

Serves 4–6

1 tbsp olive oil
100g streaky bacon, chopped
1 onion, diced
2 carrots, cut into rounds
2 celery sticks, sliced
350g combination of swede, turnip, pumpkin, parsnip or celeriac, peeled and diced
250g floury potatoes, sliced
1.5 litres well-flavoured chicken stock (see page 210)
½ small savoy cabbage, cut into thin wedges
200g cooked chicken, cut into thin strips
salt and black pepper

Lentil and spinach soup

Packed with goodness and flavour, this soup is utterly delicious.
Add a dollop of Greek yoghurt to each bowl if you like.

1 Heat the olive oil in a large saucepan and add the onion. Cook for a few minutes until the onion is starting to soften, then add the garlic and cook for another couple of minutes.

2 Sprinkle the spice over the onion and stir thoroughly. Add the mint, if using, then stir in the red lentils, making sure they are well covered with the oil and spices. Season with salt and black pepper.

3 Pour the stock into the pan and bring it to the boil. Lower the heat and simmer the soup for 25–30 minutes until the lentils have collapsed and thickened the soup. Add the spinach and stir it into the lentils until it has completely wilted.

4 Add a squeeze of lemon juice and sprinkle with herbs before serving.

Serves 4–6

2 tbsp olive oil
1 onion, sliced
2 garlic cloves, finely chopped
1 tbsp Moroccan spice mix
    (see page 213) or ras-el-hanout
½ tsp dried mint (optional)
200g red lentils
1.2 litres vegetable stock
250g spinach, chopped
lemon juice
mint or parsley, chopped
salt and black pepper

Bacon, bean and barley soup

A no-brainer. This winter staple warms you up and fills you up.

1 Heat the olive oil in a large saucepan. Add the bacon and fry until it's crisp and brown, then add the onion, carrot and celery. Cook for about 5 minutes, then add the chopped garlic and rosemary and fry for another minute.

2 Add the barley, stir briefly, then pour in the stock and season with salt and pepper. Simmer uncovered for about 45 minutes, until the vegetables and barley have softened.

3 Add the beans, tomatoes and greens and cook for another 15 minutes, until the soup has reduced down a little and the greens are completely cooked through.

4 Serve sprinkled with grated Parmesan and chopped parsley.

Serves 4–6

1 tbsp olive oil
100g smoked bacon, chopped
1 onion, chopped
1 large carrot, sliced
1 celery stick, thinly sliced
2 garlic cloves, finely chopped
sprig of rosemary
75g pearl barley
1.2 litres chicken stock
400g can of beans (borlotti or
    cannellini), drained and rinsed
3 tomatoes, roughly chopped
a bunch of kale, cavolo nero or
    other greens, chopped
Parmesan cheese, grated
chopped parsley
salt and black pepper

Ham and split pea soup

I'm loving soups and you can't beat ham and pea. I find, too, that having a soup and salad in the evening is a great way to eat if you're trying to be extra healthy and shed a few pounds. Fills you up but keeps you away from those carbs. This soup is perfect made with the cooking liquid left from boiling a ham (see page 122), but otherwise use vegetable or chicken stock or water. At one time, if I saw a mention of soaking stuff, like the peas here, I used to think it too much of a faff, but actually it's no trouble and it's worth it. You could use frozen peas instead, but the split ones taste nicer. Make double the amount of this soup while you're at it and freeze some for another day.

1 Soak the split peas in plenty of cold water overnight.

2 Melt the butter in a large saucepan. Add the onion, carrot and celery and fry them gently for 5 minutes.

3 Drain the split peas and add them to the saucepan, then pour in the stock. Bring the liquid to the boil and let it bubble away fiercely for 10 minutes, then turn the heat down to a gentle simmer. Taste for seasoning and add salt and pepper as required – the ham stock will be salty so you might not need any salt.

4 Simmer for about an hour or until the peas are tender. Whizz the soup with a hand blender a few times in the saucepan or purée half the soup in a blender or food processor – it's good to keep some texture. Add the diced or shredded ham and heat through, then sprinkle with parsley and serve piping hot.

- -

Davina's tip
Home-made soup is a million times tastier and healthier than shop-bought versions – even the fancy expensive ones – which may contain lots of salt and even sugar. Make a big pot of soup and stash it in the fridge for quick lunches, to take to work and reheat, or for a speedy supper with some cheese and salad. Soups freeze well too.

Serves 4–6

400g green split peas
25g butter
1 onion, finely chopped
1 carrot, finely diced
1 celery stick, finely diced
1.5 litres ham stock (or vegetable or chicken)
100g cooked ham, finely diced or shredded
handful of parsley, chopped
salt and black pepper

Salmon niçoise

Hot-smoked salmon rocks! It's chunkier than regular smoked salmon and crumbles into succulent flakes so makes a great addition to this variation on the classic salad niçoise.

1 Put the potatoes in a pan of lightly salted water, bring them to the boil and cook them for about 15 minutes, or until tender.

2 Put the lettuce in a large salad bowl. Trim the green beans – just pinch off the stalks but leave the whiskery tails in place.

3 Bring another saucepan of water to the boil. Add the eggs, then after 3 minutes add the beans and cook for another 4 minutes. Drain immediately and run everything under cold water. Leave the beans to cool completely, then add them to the lettuce. Peel the eggs and cut them in half.

4 Add the potatoes, olives and cherry tomatoes to the salad bowl. Mix the salad dressing ingredients together and season with salt and black pepper.

5 Pour two-thirds of the dressing over the contents of the salad bowl. Add the eggs and salmon, then drizzle over the rest of the dressing and serve immediately.

Serves 4

400g baby new potatoes
1 romaine lettuce heart, thickly
    shredded
200g green beans
4 eggs
100g black olives, pitted
12 cherry tomatoes, halved
200g hot-smoked salmon, broken
    into chunks

Dressing
3 tbsp olive oil
1 tbsp lemon juice
1 tsp balsamic vinegar
½ tsp mustard
salt and black pepper

Feta, watermelon and avocado salad

Chunks of watermelon are amazing in a salad, bringing a gorgeously sweet crunchiness. Combine that with salty feta and ripe avocado and you have a feast that's as lovely to eat as it is to look at.

1 Cut the watermelon into chunks, removing the peel and seeds. Do this over a bowl to catch any juice and set the juice aside.

2 Put the salad leaves in a bowl or on a serving platter and add the watermelon, avocados, radishes and feta.

3 Whisk together any watermelon juice with the lime juice and olive oil, then season with salt and pepper. Drizzle this dressing over the salad and garnish with a few sprigs of mint.

Serves 4

½ small watermelon (about 500g)
salad leaves (lamb's lettuce, rocket or baby leaves)
2 avocados, peeled, stoned and cut into small chunks
small bunch of radishes, halved
150g feta, cut into small cubes
juice of 1 lime
2 tbsp olive oil
a few sprigs of mint
salt and black pepper

Roast vegetable and couscous salad

You'll notice that this is made with barley couscous. Regular couscous is made from wheat but this barley version is even better – and perfect if you're wheat intolerant. It's available in supermarkets and prepared just like any other couscous. This salad is lovely with my slow-roast Moroccan lamb (see page 124) and soaks up the yummy juices. Good on its own too.

1 Preheat the oven to 200°C/180°C Fan/Gas 6. Line a roasting tray with foil.

2 Spread the vegetables over the tray and drizzle them with olive oil. Season the vegetables with salt and pepper, then roast them in the oven for about 30 minutes. They should be soft and starting to brown around the edges. Remove the veg from the oven and leave them to cool slightly.

3 Put the couscous in a bowl, pour over 400ml boiling water and add the butter, lemon juice and zest. Season with salt and pepper, then cover and leave the couscous to stand for at least 5 minutes. It should absorb all the liquid. Fluff it up with a fork, add the herbs and pile the roasted veg on top.

4 Sprinkle with some torn basil before serving. This salad is also nice served on a bed of salad leaves.

Serves 4

1 red onion, diced
1 courgette, diced
1 red pepper, diced
1 sweet potato, peeled and diced
2–3 tbsp olive oil
200g barley couscous
25g butter
juice and zest of ½ lemon
plenty of chopped herbs, such
   as coriander, parsley or mint
a few basil leaves, to serve
salt and black pepper

Warm quinoa salad with avocado and broad beans

For ages I avoided quinoa – partly because I didn't know how to say it! But since I've discovered how good it is and how easy it is to cook I use it more often than couscous. This is an amazing salad, with beautiful fresh flavours from the herbs and beans and velvety texture from the avocado. For the record – I used to say kwinn-OH-ah, but now I know it should be KEEN-wah. So there you go. And it's in all the supermarkets now.

1 First cook the quinoa. Rinse it well, then put it in a saucepan and cover with 150ml water. Season with salt, bring it to the boil, then turn down the heat and cover the pan with a lid. Simmer the quinoa until all the water has been absorbed. Remove the pan from the heat and set it aside with the lid on so the quinoa steams and keeps warm.

2 Bring a saucepan of water to the boil, add the broad beans and cook them for 2–3 minutes. Drain and run the beans under cold water. If any of them are on the large side, remove the greyish outer skins to reveal the bright green beans.

3 Mix all the salad dressing ingredients together.

4 Arrange the salad leaves in a serving bowl. Mix the quinoa with two-thirds of the beans, avocado, spring onions and tomatoes and spoon it over the salad leaves. Add the remaining ingredients on top and pour over the dressing. Finish with the fresh herbs.

- -

Davina's tip
I often cook my quinoa in chicken stock for extra flavour.

Serves 4

75g quinoa
200g broad beans (fresh or frozen)
salad leaves
1 avocado, peeled, stoned and
    cut into chunks
4 spring onions, sliced into
    rounds
a few cherry tomatoes, halved
handful of fresh mint and
    coriander leaves
salt

Dressing
1 tbsp rice wine vinegar
1 tbsp soy sauce or tamari
½ tsp grated ginger
pinch of ground cumin (optional)
½ tsp honey
½ tsp sesame oil

Rainbow salad

Another corker of a salad. Whenever I'm asked to bring a salad to a party I take this one and it's universally loved. I like the American style of chopping everything quite small like this so you can eat it just with a fork – again, ideal for a party. BTW, I always use frozen sweetcorn, rather than canned, as it has no added sugar or salt and the kernels tend to be fatter and juicier. Also you can use as much or as little as you like rather than having to use up a whole can. The dressing is also American style and based on the ever popular ranch dressing, which contains buttermilk.

1 Put the chopped bacon in a dry pan and fry until it's all crisp and brown. Set aside.

2 Arrange all the remaining salad ingredients in a serving dish. You can do this in a variety of ways – either combine them free-form, or layer them up in a bowl or a glass dish, starting with the lettuce at the bottom. Finish with the chicken, then sprinkle the bacon over the top.

3 Now make the dressing. If you're using milk and lemon juice, mix them together and leave to stand for 5 minutes until the mixture has thickened. Then whisk this, or the buttermilk, with the rest of dressing ingredients and season with salt and black pepper. Drizzle the dressing over the salad and serve immediately.

Serves 4

4 rashers of smoked streaky bacon, finely chopped
2 little gems or 1 romaine lettuce heart, shredded
1 large carrot, grated
1 large or 2 small beetroots, grated
¼ white cabbage, finely shredded
¼ cucumber, diced
150g sweetcorn
200g cooked chicken, diced

Dressing
150ml buttermilk (or 150ml whole milk and 2 tsp lemon juice)
1 tbsp mayonnaise
1 tbsp soured cream or crème fraiche
1 tbsp finely chopped herbs
1 garlic clove
½ tsp mustard (optional)
salt and black pepper

Halloumi, watercress and pomegranate salad

I love, love, love halloumi cheese and it's perfect in this salad. Soaking the onion is a great tip that I learned while working on this book so do try it. This really does remove any bitterness so you can appreciate the lovely sweet flavour of the onion. Supermarkets sell pomegranate molasses now but if you don't have any, just use honey.

1 Soak the red onion slices in a bowl of cold water for 10 minutes while you prepare the rest of the ingredients.

2 Heat a griddle pan on a medium to high heat until smoking. Add the slices of halloumi cheese and grill them for a couple of minutes on each side until slightly softened and marked with char lines from the griddle. If you don't have a griddle pan, you could cook the halloumi under a hot grill.

3 Arrange the watercress on a platter or salad bowl and sprinkle the lentils on top. Drain the red onions and sprinkle those over too, then add the slices of halloumi.

4 Whisk all the dressing ingredients together and season with salt and pepper. Drizzle the dressing over the salad, then sprinkle with the pomegranate seeds and mint.

- -

Davina's tip
Here's how to remove the seeds from a pomegranate. Roll the fruit on your work surface a few times – this helps to loosen the seeds inside – then cut the pomegranate in half. Hold one half over a bowl, cut-side down, and bash the skin with a wooden spoon. The seeds will fall out into the bowl.

Serves 4

½ red onion, sliced
250g halloumi cheese, sliced
100g watercress, washed and
    drained
400g can of lentils (about 240g
    drained weight)
seeds from ½ pomegranate
large handful of mint

Dressing
3 tbsp olive oil
1 tbsp lemon juice
1 tbsp pomegranate molasses
    or ½ tsp honey
salt and black pepper

Red slaw

What can I say? This always goes down well and when I make it, people always ask me for the recipe. I sometimes include a little white cabbage, which looks pretty with the red. The apple and hazelnuts add a lovely touch of sweetness.

1 Shred the red cabbage as finely as you can, making sure the strands aren't too long. Mix the cabbage with the other vegetables and apple in a large salad bowl.

2 If using the hazelnuts, toast them in a dry frying pan for a minute, shaking them constantly, until they've turned very light brown. Don't take your eyes off them for a second, as they burn easily. Chop the toasted nuts roughly and set them aside.

3 Whisk the dressing ingredients together in a small jug and season with salt and pepper.

4 Pour the dressing over the vegetables and mix thoroughly. Sprinkle over the nuts, if using, and leave the slaw to stand for a few minutes before eating.

Serves 4

300g red cabbage (about
   ½ medium cabbage)
1 raw beetroot, washed and grated
2 carrots, grated
1 small onion, finely chopped
1 apple, peeled and grated
25g hazelnuts (optional), halved
   or roughly chopped

Dressing
2 tbsp mayonnaise (see page 210)
1 tbsp crème fraiche
1 tsp cider or white wine vinegar
¼ tsp sweet smoked paprika
   (optional)
1 tsp wholegrain mustard
   (optional)
salt and black pepper

Bean salad

Quick and easy to make, this classic combo of fresh beans and pulses is always popular. It's great with runner beans too, when they're in season.

1 Bring a saucepan of water to the boil, add the green beans and cook them for 3 minutes. Drain and refresh them under cold water.

2 Put the green beans, canned beans, tomatoes, red onion and cucumber in a bowl and mix them all together. Whisk the lemon juice, olive oil, mustard and honey in a small jug and pour this over the salad.

3 Scatter over some basil leaves and shavings of Parmesan cheese just before serving.

Serves 4

400g green beans
400g can of borlotti or cannellini
  beans, drained and rinsed
200g cherry tomatoes, halved
1 small red onion, diced
½ cucumber, diced
juice of ½ lemon
2 tbsp olive oil
½ tsp mustard
½ tsp honey
handful of fresh basil leaves
Parmesan cheese shavings

Potato salad

My lovely sister Caroline was never without a jar of cornichons in her fridge and they are an essential for potato salad in my house. Everyone loves a potato salad and you can add extras if you like, such as smoked fish or garlicky sausage. Keep the skins on the potatoes for extra fibre.

1 Cut up any of the larger potatoes, leaving baby-sized ones whole. Put the potatoes in a saucepan and cover with water. Bring the water to the boil, add a pinch of salt, then simmer the potatoes for 15–20 minutes until tender.

2 Mix the mayonnaise with the crème fraiche and vinegar or lemon juice in a small jug. Season with salt and pepper.

3 Drain the potatoes and allow them to cool slightly. Put them in a bowl with the spring onions, cornichons and dill, then stir in the dressing. Toss the salad very lightly and leave it to stand for 10 minutes or so for the flavours to blend. Serve warm or chilled.

Serves 4

1kg new waxy potatoes, unpeeled
2 tbsp Davina's mayonnaise
  (see page 210)
1 tbsp crème fraiche
1 tsp white wine vinegar or
  lemon juice
6 spring onions, sliced in rounds
a few small cornichons, sliced
a few sprigs of dill, chopped
salt and black pepper

Pea, pesto and spelt salad

Spelt is just another type of wheat and it's easier to digest and better for you than regular wheat. It's used to make flour, but you can also buy packets of pre-cooked wholegrain spelt in supermarkets and it's a great ingredient to have on hand for a quick salad like this one. The little grains have a nice firm texture and a slightly sweet flavour that goes beautifully with the pesto. The blue cheese makes the perfect finishing touch. Love it.

1 First make the pesto, by blitzing all the ingredients together in a food processor or blender. Season with salt and pepper.

2 Cook the peas in boiling water for 2 minutes, then drain them and set aside.

3 Put half the pesto in a mixing bowl and add the spelt, peas and mint leaves and mix. Gently stir in the salad leaves and crumble over the blue cheese, if using. Season with salt and pepper and drizzle over more olive oil and lemon juice if you like. You could also add more of the pesto, or save it for another dish.

Serves 4

100g peas (frozen or fresh)
250g ready-cooked spelt
handful of fresh mint leaves
100g salad leaves, such as rocket and watercress, or a bag of mixed leaves
100g Gorgonzola, Dolcelatte or other blue cheese, roughly cubed (optional)
salt and black pepper

Pesto
50g fresh basil leaves
25g pine nuts
40g Pecorino or Parmesan cheese, grated
1 garlic clove, crushed
zest and juice of 1 lemon
6 tbsp extra virgin olive oil

Davina's favourites

4 **Main Meals**

"Roast chicken would probably be my desert island meal. I could eat it for ever. And there's no white flour or packaged stuff in my gravy."

Roast tomato pasta

Another recipe to help deal with the triffid-like tomato plants in our greenhouse. And let's talk about spelt pasta. I was terrified of it, to be honest, but it's perfectly easy to deal with. I think it's even better than the wholewheat pasta I used to use – tastes slightly lighter and less worthy but still contains plenty of nutrients and fibre.

1 Preheat the oven to 180°C/160°C Fan/Gas 4.

2 Cut the tomatoes in half and put them in a roasting tin with the garlic cloves. Season well with salt and black pepper, then drizzle over the olive oil and sprinkle with the herbs. Place the tomatoes and garlic in the oven and roast for an hour. By this point the garlic should be soft and the tomatoes starting to caramelise.

3 Remove the tin from the oven and leave the tomatoes and garlic to cool for a while. As soon as the tomatoes are cool enough to handle, slip off the skins and discard them.

4 Put the cream cheese or goat's cheese into a bowl. Mash it up slightly, then add the peeled tomatoes and any juices from the roasting tin. Squeeze the flesh out of the garlic cloves into the bowl, discarding the skins, then mix everything together thoroughly.

5 Cook the pasta in plenty of boiling water according to the packet instructions. Add the spinach for the last minute – it will wilt down immediately – and drain everything well.

6 Mix the pasta with the tomato and cream cheese sauce. Add a squeeze of lemon juice and the Parmesan, then mix thoroughly, separating any clumps of spinach where necessary. Serve with more Parmesan and torn basil leaves.

Serves 4

6 large, very ripe tomatoes (about 600g)
1 head of garlic, cloves separated but unpeeled
2 tbsp olive oil
a few sprigs of thyme or ½ tsp dried herbs
150g cream cheese or soft goat's cheese
250g spelt or wholewheat pasta
200g fresh spinach
a squeeze of lemon juice
15g Parmesan cheese, finely grated, plus extra to serve
a handful of basil leaves
salt and black pepper

Barley risotto with mushrooms and butternut squash

I love a risotto and barley is a wonderful alternative to ordinary rice now that I'm following my healthy eating plan. There's nothing complicated about barley and it soaks up flavours in the same way as rice. You could also make this risotto with spelt.

1 Heat the olive oil and half the butter in a large saucepan. Gently fry the onion and garlic for 2 minutes, then add the mushrooms and butternut squash. Continue to cook for about 5 minutes until the mushrooms are collapsing down and everything is softening.

2 Add the barley or spelt, then the sage and season with salt and pepper. Stir well.

3 Pour in the stock and bring it to the boil. Turn down the heat and simmer gently, stirring regularly, until most of the liquid has been absorbed and the barley is tender.

4 Beat in the rest of the butter with the Parmesan until the risotto is creamy. Serve with more grated Parmesan.

Serves 4

1 tbsp olive oil
50g butter
1 onion, finely chopped
1 garlic clove, finely chopped
400g mixed mushrooms, wiped
  clean and finely sliced
200g butternut squash, peeled
  and diced
250g pearl barley (or spelt)
½ tsp dried sage or 1 tbsp
  chopped fresh sage
1 litre chicken or vegetable stock
25g Parmesan cheese, grated,
  plus extra Parmesan to serve
salt and black pepper

Risotto with spring vegetables

I like to make this classic spring vegetable risotto, known as risotto primavera, with brown risotto rice, instead of white, for a healthier dish. It works brilliantly but you really do need to soak the rice overnight before using it, trust me. I did try skipping this step and the rice took ages to cook and after all, there's nothing that difficult about soaking. If you fancy, add 100ml of wine after you've fried the onion, courgette and garlic, and before adding the stock. Wine does up the sugar content though.

1 Drain the soaked rice.

2 Heat the olive oil and butter in a very wide, straight-sided pan. When the butter is foaming, add the onion, courgette and garlic and fry gently for a few minutes. The courgette will disintegrate, but don't worry – it adds creaminess to the dish. Add the rice and cook for another couple of minutes, then pour in all the chicken stock.

3 Bring the stock to the boil, turn the heat right down to a slow simmer and cover the pan. Simmer the risotto gently for about 45 minutes – keep checking regularly and give it a quick stir. At the end of the cooking time, taste for seasoning and add salt and pepper if necessary.

4 When the rice is almost ready, bring a saucepan of water to the boil. Add the asparagus and cook for a minute. Add the peas and cook for another minute, then add the spinach to the pan. As soon as the spinach has wilted down, drain everything thoroughly.

5 When the risotto is cooked to your liking, stir in the vegetables and lemon zest. Finally, add the butter and Parmesan and beat thoroughly until they have completely melted into the risotto and the risotto is lovely and creamy. Stir in lots of fresh basil.

6 Serve with extra Parmesan cheese to add at the table.

Serves 4

250g brown risotto rice or brown
   short-grain rice, soaked overnight
1 tbsp olive oil
10g butter
1 onion, finely chopped
1 courgette, finely diced or grated
2 garlic cloves, finely chopped
750g chicken stock (see page 210)
bunch of asparagus (about 200g),
   cut into 5cm pieces
150g peas, fresh or frozen
100g spinach
1 tsp lemon zest
salt and black pepper

To finish
25g butter
25g Parmesan cheese, grated,
   plus extra to serve
handful of fresh basil

Fish and chips

This is all about the batter and my batter is made with chickpea flour, which gives a nice light crispy coating. A bit of spice is nice so I like to add my spice blend, but you can leave this out if you prefer. Yes, it is a bit of work, compared with nipping to the chippy, but well worth the effort.

1 Start by making the tartare sauce. Simply mix all the ingredients together in a bowl and season with salt and black pepper. Chill until ready to serve.

2 Next, get the chips in the oven. Preheat the oven to 200°C/180°C Fan/Gas 6. Cut the potatoes into thick wedges, leaving the skin on. Put the wedges in a large saucepan and cover them with water. Bring the water to the boil and cook the potatoes for 2 minutes, then drain and dry them off as much as possible.

3 Arrange the potato wedges on a large baking tray and drizzle over the vegetable oil, making sure all the potatoes are covered. Sprinkle with salt and cook in the preheated oven for about 45 minutes.

4 To make the batter for the fish, sieve the chickpea flour in a bowl with the spice blend, if using, and half a teaspoon of salt. Whisk in the water or beer to make a smooth batter.

5 When the chips are nearly ready, heat the oil for cooking the fish in a deep-fryer or a large saucepan and test the heat with a cube of bread. The oil is ready when the cube of bread takes about 30 seconds to crisp up and turn an even golden brown. Please be extra careful when deep-frying and never leave a pan of hot oil unattended.

6 Spread some chickpea flour on a plate. Dust a couple of fish fillets in flour, then dip them in the batter. Carefully drop the fish into the oil and fry until crisp and brown – this will take about 3 minutes. Drain the fried fish on kitchen towel. Fry the rest of the fish in the same way and serve immediately with the chips and tartare sauce.

Davina's tip
Chickpea flour is also sometimes known as gram flour and you can buy it in supermarkets.

Serves 4

Fish
100g chickpea flour, well sieved, plus extra for dusting
1 tsp Davina's spice blend (see page 213)
150ml chilled water or beer
vegetable oil to half fill a deep-fryer or a large saucepan
4 fish fillets, about 150–200g each
salt and black pepper

Chips
1kg floury potatoes, such as Maris Pipers or King Edwards (unpeeled)
2–3 tbsp vegetable oil

Tartare sauce
150g Davina's mayonnaise (see page 210)
1 tbsp capers, finely chopped
grated zest and juice of ½ lime
a small bunch of coriander, finely chopped, including stems
1 mild green chilli, deseeded and finely chopped (optional)

Salmon with lentils

This is a quick and easy one-pot supper and a brilliantly simple way to cook fish. Puy lentils are available in most supermarkets.

1 Preheat the oven to 180°C/160°C Fan/Gas 4.

2 Heat the olive oil in a roasting tin on the hob and add the slices of leek. Fry them for a few minutes until they're starting to soften, but don't let them brown. Stir in the garlic, thyme leaves, lemon zest and puy lentils and cook for another minute.

3 Pour in the chicken stock and season with salt and black pepper, then bring everything to the boil. Cover the tin with foil and carefully put it in the oven for about 30 minutes.

4 At the end of this time, remove the tin from the oven, take off the foil and check that the lentils are nearly cooked – if they're not quite tender enough, pop them back in the oven for a few more minutes. Stir the mustard and lemon juice into the lentils.

5 Season the salmon fillets with salt and pepper and place them on top of the lentils. Dot a few cherry tomatoes around them. Put the tin back in the oven for 8–10 minutes until the salmon is just cooked through – it should still be slightly pink in the middle. Sprinkle with parsley before serving.

- -

Davina's tip
Unless you buy organic lemons, which are more expensive, the skin will be coated with wax and pesticides. Give your lemons a good scrub in hot water and dry them well before zesting.

Serves 4

2 tbsp olive oil
1 leek, sliced into thin rounds
1 garlic clove, finely chopped
1 tsp finely chopped thyme
   leaves or ½ tsp dried herbs
zest of ½ lemon
200g puy lentils, rinsed
500ml chicken stock (see page 210)
1 tsp Dijon mustard
juice of ½ lemon
4 salmon fillets, skinned
a few cherry tomatoes
handful of chopped parsley
salt and black pepper

Sea bass with mushrooms and potatoes

Lots of people, me included, get stressed about pan-frying fish. It looks so easy on 'Masterchef' but when I try it, the skin sticks to the pan and I end up in a mess. This recipe, though, is a doddle. The fish is cooked in the oven on a luxurious bed of potatoes and mushrooms and you have a delicious meal with no tricky stuff. It's important to spread the potatoes and mushrooms out well in a large roasting tin so they brown and don't steam.

1 Preheat the oven to 200°C/180°C Fan/Gas 6.

2 Put the potatoes in a saucepan and cover them with water. Bring the water to the boil and simmer the potatoes for 7–8 minutes, until they're half way to being cooked through. Drain and slice them thickly.

3 Take a large roasting tin and line it with foil if you like. Add the potatoes and mushrooms, spreading them out evenly in a single layer. Drizzle over the olive oil, then add the thyme or lemon thyme, garlic and lemon juice and zest. Season generously.

4 Roast the mushrooms and potatoes in the oven for about 15 minutes, by which time they should be browning around the edges.

5 Rub the skin of the sea bass fillets with olive oil, then season them with salt and pepper. Place the fillets on top of the mushrooms and potatoes, skin-side up, and put the tin back in the oven. Roast for 8–10 minutes, depending on the thickness of the fillets, until the fish is just cooked through. Serve immediately.

- -

Davina's tip
This is a lovely easy way to do fish for a supper party, as you can get the potatoes and mushrooms prepared and cook the fish when everyone has arrived. There's no slaving over a hot frying pan and more time for chit-chat.

Serves 4

600g new potatoes, unpeeled
400g mushrooms (a mixture is good), thickly sliced
75ml olive oil, plus extra for rubbing on the fish
a few sprigs of thyme, or lemon thyme if you can get it
3 garlic cloves, finely chopped
juice and grated zest of ½ lemon
4 sea bass fillets, 100–150g each
salt and black pepper

Fish patties

These are not fish cakes – no potato – but a lighter sort of fish patty that you can also make into little balls or sliders. If you want a bit more bite to your patties, try adding some wasabi or mustard to the mixture.

1 Rinse the quinoa well, then put it in a saucepan with 150ml of water. Bring it to the boil, cover, then simmer on a low heat until all the water is absorbed. Take the pan off the heat but leave it to stand with the lid on so the quinoa dries out nicely as it cools.

2 Roughly dice the fish and put it in the freezer for about 20 minutes to chill thoroughly.

3 Take the fish out of the freezer, put it in a food processor and pulse until coarsely ground – freezing it first gives a better texture and stops the fish turning to a mush.

4 Tip the fish into a bowl and add the other ingredients, except the sesame seeds – you might not need all the quinoa, so add about two-thirds of it at first. If the mixture seems too sloppy, add the rest. Season generously with salt and pepper and mix thoroughly. Chill the mixture for another half an hour.

5 Preheat the oven to 220°C/200°C Fan/Gas 7. Line a baking tray with baking parchment.

6 Divide the mixture, according to how you want to serve it. It might be quite sloppy but don't worry, just shape it as best you can. For patties, shape the mixture into about 6. For sliders, divide it into 8. For fish balls, make 20 balls about the size of a golfball.

7 Pour the sesame seeds on to a plate and roll the fish patties, sliders or balls in them until well coated.

8 Place the fish patties, sliders or balls on the baking tray. Cook for 8–12 minutes, depending on size and how well done you like your fish.

9 Serve however you like, but these are great with the wasabi mayonnaise. Simply combine a portion of Davina's mayonnaise with wasabi paste, lime zest and juice. Also good served with home-made ketchup (see page 212) on the side.

Makes 6 patties, 8 sliders or 20 fish balls

50g quinoa
500g tuna or salmon fillets, skinned
2 garlic cloves, finely chopped
10g fresh root ginger, peeled and grated
2 tbsp finely chopped fresh coriander
grated zest and juice of 1 lime
1 tbsp soy or fish sauce
1 egg
1 tsp sesame oil
a mixture of black and white sesame seeds, for coating
salt and black pepper

Wasabi mayonnaise (optional)
portion of Davina's mayonnaise (see page 210)
½ tsp wasabi paste
grated zest and juice of ½ lime

Fish pie

The topping on this fish pie is a nod to gratin dauphinoise – a creamy sliced potato dish that's a favourite of mine. I've suggested keeping the skin on the potatoes so you get the full benefit of their nutrients and fibre. Fish pie is always a treat and this is an easy one to make. You can replace some of the milk with white wine, but remember that wine contains sugar.

1 Preheat the oven to 180°C/160°C Fan/Gas 4.

2 Put the potatoes for the topping in a saucepan, cover them with water and bring to the boil. Simmer them for 10 minutes until partly cooked, then drain and refresh in cold water. Cut the potatoes into slices of about ½ cm and set aside.

3 Make the béchamel sauce as on page 211. Remove the pan from the heat and stir in all the parsley, dill or chives.

4 Put the fish in a fairly shallow 2-litre ovenproof dish and sprinkle over the raw prawns and chopped eggs. Pour the béchamel over the fish and fold everything together gently so the fish gets completely covered in the sauce.

5 Arrange the slices of potato on top of the pie and brush them with melted butter. Bake the pie in the oven for 40–45 minutes, until the potatoes are browned and the filling is piping hot. Serve with some peas on the side.

Serves 4–6

600g fish fillets (salmon, cod, smoked haddock), skinned and little bones removed
150g raw shelled prawns
2 eggs, hard-boiled for 8 minutes, peeled and finely chopped

Béchamel sauce
50g butter
50g wholemeal spelt flour
500ml whole milk
large handful of parsley, dill or chives, finely chopped
salt and black pepper

Topping
500g floury potatoes, unpeeled
20g butter, melted

Davina's roast chicken

Roast chicken would probably be my desert island meal. I could eat it for ever. For me, Sunday is family day and roast day. Roast chicken is the family's favourite and that's why I love it so much – it reminds of me of my family. For a real treat, buy free-range if you can. It just tastes better.

1 Take the chicken out of the fridge at least half an hour before you want to cook it, so it can come to room temperature. Take the butter out of the fridge too. Preheat the oven to 190°C/170°C Fan/Gas 5.

2 Make the stuffing. Heat the olive oil in a frying pan. Add the onion and celery and cook them for several minutes over a medium heat until softened. Remove the pan from the heat and add the sage and lemon zest. Take the skin off the sausages and crumble the meat into a bowl with the wholemeal breadcrumbs. Add the onion mixture and the egg, then season with salt and pepper and mix everything thoroughly – it's easiest to do this with your hands.

3 Divide the stuffing between the neck end of the chicken and the cavity, then put the chicken in a roasting tin. Smear butter all over the chicken skin and season with salt and pepper. Squeeze the lemon juice over the chicken too.

4 Pour 300ml of wine, stock or water around the chicken, then roast in the preheated oven. The timing depends on the weight of the chicken. It needs 20 minutes for every 500g, plus another 20 minutes at the end. So for a 1.5kg bird, that's 1 hour and 20 minutes. Turn the heat up to 220°C/200°C Fan/Gas 7 for the last 15 minutes to crisp up the skin.

5 Remove the chicken from the oven and check that it's done by piercing the thickest part of the thigh with a skewer. It's ready if the juices are running clear and the leg feels loose enough to pull away easily. If it's not quite done, pop it back in the oven for 5 minutes or so. Put the chicken on a warm dish, then cover it in foil and leave it to rest while you make the gravy.

6 Put the roasting tin on the hob and bring the cooking juices to the boil, scraping up any brown bits sticking to the bottom. Whisk to mix the liquid and fat in the tin, so you end up with a thin well-flavoured gravy. Pour this into a warm gravy boat or jug.

7 Serve the chicken with spoonfuls of stuffing and the gravy, plus some lovely roast potatoes (see page 146).

Serves 4

1 chicken, about 1.5kg in weight
25g butter, at room temperature
juice of ½ a lemon
300ml white wine, chicken stock
(see page 210) or water
salt and black pepper

Stuffing
1 tbsp olive oil
1 small onion, finely chopped
1 celery stick, finely chopped
1 tsp dried sage or 1 tbsp fresh
grated zest of 1 lemon
2 pork sausages
75g wholemeal breadcrumbs
1 egg

Glazed chicken wings

My husband loves chicken wings and they remind him of Virginia – a place we both know and love and often visit to see family. I find it easiest to leave the wings whole and just remove the tips – the smallest bit that ends in a point. You can cut these off and use them in stock. Some wings come with tips already removed.

1 Blitz all the marinade ingredients in a blender or food processor to make a fairly smooth paste. Rub this over the wings and put them on a wire rack. Leave the wings to marinate in the fridge for at least a couple of hours, or overnight.

2 Preheat the oven to 180°C/160°C Fan/Gas 4. Remove the wings from the fridge and allow them to come to room temperature. Place the wire rack in a roasting tin and roast the wings for 30 minutes.

3 Turn the oven up to 200C/180C Fan/Gas 6.

4 Mix the oil with the teriyaki sauce to make the glaze. Remove the wings from the oven and brush them with glaze, then sprinkle over a few sesame seeds. Roast the wings for another 20 minutes until they're well browned and glossy. Yummy!

Serves 4–6

1kg chicken wings, tips removed
1 tbsp vegetable oil or melted
   butter
2 tbsp teriyaki sauce (see page 213)
sprinkling of sesame seeds,
   to serve

Marinade
1 onion, chopped
2 garlic cloves, peeled
5cm fresh root ginger, peeled
1 tbsp soy sauce
juice of 1 lemon
1 tsp salt

Chicken pot pie

This is another meal that pleases my husband greatly. Everyone loves a pie and for me, chicken is the king of pies. Poached chicken is so beautifully succulent and tender, and the leeks and carrots add a lovely sweetness. It's a dish that shows that healthy can be delicious.

1 Put the carrots in a large saucepan and add the stock or water, then the tarragon and garlic cloves. Bring to the boil, then turn down the heat and simmer for 10 minutes.

2 Add the chicken to the pan. Put the leeks in a steamer basket and suspend it above the chicken, then cover and simmer gently for about 10 minutes.

3 Make the pastry. Put the flour in a bowl with the salt and rub in the butter and cream cheese with your hands. Add the milk gradually until you have a smooth dough that comes together easily. Wrap the dough in cling film and chill it in the fridge for at least half an hour.

4 Strain the chicken and vegetables, reserving the cooking liquor. Remove the garlic cloves from the liquor and set them aside. Measure out 500ml of liquid and use this to make the béchamel sauce as on page 211. Stir in the cream or crème fraiche, then squeeze the flesh out of the garlic cloves and add this to the béchamel. Discard the garlic skins. Season the sauce with salt and pepper.

5 Cut the chicken into bite-sized pieces and put them in a 2-litre pie dish with the carrots, leeks and mushrooms. Put a pie bird in the centre if you have one. Pour the sauce over the chicken and vegetables and leave to cool.

6 Preheat the oven to 200°C/180°C Fan/Gas 6.

7 Roll out the pastry on floured work surface and use it to cover the pie. Trim the edges and crimp them with your fingers, then brush the pastry with beaten egg.

8 Bake the pie in the preheated oven for 35–40 minutes until the pastry is a deep golden brown and the filling is piping hot.

Serves 6

200g carrots (about 3), cut into large dice
500ml chicken stock (see page 210) or water
large sprig of tarragon
½ head garlic, cloves left unpeeled
600g chicken thigh fillets or a mixture of chicken thighs and breasts, boned and skinned
3 leeks, cut into 2cm rounds
1 quantity of béchamel sauce (see page 211), made with 500ml of chicken poaching liquid
2 tbsp double cream or crème fraiche
250g button mushrooms, halved
salt and black pepper

Pastry
200g wholemeal spelt flour
pinch of salt
75g cold butter, diced
75g cream cheese
1–2 tbsp milk
1 egg, beaten, for glazing

Yoghurt-marinated chicken

My eldest daughter is the marinater in our household and loves making marinades and rubs. This recipe is right up her street. As she has found, there's nothing difficult about marinating – you just have to remember to do it! This chicken is perfect with the herby rice.

1 Mix all the marinade ingredients together in a large bowl. Using a sharp knife, cut slashes into the chicken at intervals. Add the chicken to the bowl with the marinade and massage the mixture into the cuts. Cover the bowl with cling film and leave it in the fridge for a few hours or overnight.

2 To cook the chicken, preheat the oven to its highest setting. Line a baking tray with foil. Remove the chicken from the marinade, scraping off any excess, and space the pieces evenly on the baking tray.

3 Put the chicken in the oven and immediately turn the heat down to 200°C/180°C Fan/Gas 6. Bake the chicken for about 40 minutes, or until the juices run clear in the thickest part of the meat when pierced with a skewer and the flesh has started to char in places. Serve the chicken with herby brown rice and a green salad.

Serves 4

8 chicken pieces, on the bone, skinned
wedges of lime, to serve

Marinade
200ml plain yoghurt
juice and zest of 1 lemon
1 small onion, finely chopped or grated
2 garlic cloves, crushed
5g fresh root ginger, finely grated
2 tsp Davina's spice blend (see page 213) or mild curry powder
½–1 tsp chilli powder (optional)

Herby brown rice

1 Rinse the brown rice and soak it in fresh cold water for 1 hour. Tip it into a sieve and drain thoroughly.

2 Heat the oil in a large saucepan. Add the onion and garlic and fry gently for just a couple of minutes, then stir in the drained rice. Stir for another couple of minutes until the rice is well coated with oil, then pour the stock into the pan. Add the cinnamon stick and bay leaves and season with salt and pepper.

3 Bring the stock to the boil, then cover the pan and turn the heat down to its lowest setting. Cook for about 25 minutes until all the liquid has absorbed and the rice is cooked through but still has a slight bite.

4 Remove the pan from the heat and take out the cinnamon stick and bay leaves, then stir all the fresh herbs into the rice. Serve immediately.

Serves 4

250g brown rice
2 tbsp olive oil
1 small onion, finely chopped
2 garlic cloves, finely chopped
500ml chicken stock (see page 210)
5cm piece of cinnamon stick
2 bay leaves
large handfuls of fresh coriander, parsley and mint
salt and black pepper

Chicken with chorizo, chickpeas and kale

For time, ease and washing up, I love a one-pot and I love anything with chorizo. Kale is the new broccoli – everybody's doing it – but you can use other greens, as long as they keep their shape and don't go mushy. Spinach doesn't work. Two cans of chickpeas might be slightly too much, but one isn't enough I find, so open two and save any leftovers for a salad.

1 Preheat the oven to 200°C/180°C Fan/Gas 6.

2 Heat the oil in a large casserole dish that can go on the hob. Add the chicken thighs or pieces and brown them thoroughly on both sides. Make sure the skin in particular is crisp and brown. Remove the chicken from the dish and set it aside, then pour off the excess fat released by the chicken.

3 Add the slices of chorizo to the casserole dish and brown them for a couple of minutes on each side. Remove them from the dish and again drain off any excess fat. Add the onion to the casserole dish and fry gently for 5 minutes, then add the garlic and cook for another minute.

4 Add the chickpeas (as many of them as you want) and tomatoes, then stir well to combine. Tuck in the sprig of thyme, pour over the chicken stock and season with salt and pepper. Pile the kale on top of the chickpeas, then arrange the chicken and chorizo on top. Season with salt and pepper again.

5 Put the lid on the casserole dish or cover it with foil and place the dish in the oven for 20 minutes. Then remove the lid and cook for a further 15 minutes or until the chicken is completely cooked through.

Serves 4

1 tbsp olive oil
8 chicken thighs and/or legs, with skin and bone
2 cooking chorizo sausages, sliced into rounds
1 onion, sliced
2 garlic cloves, finely chopped
2 x 400g cans of chickpeas, drained and rinsed
1 x 400g can of chopped tomatoes
large sprig of thyme
200ml chicken stock (see page 210)
small bunch of kale, thickly shredded
salt and black pepper

Pot-roast chicken

There's a lovely French touch to this, with the little onions or shallots and the mushrooms. The chicken is infused with wonderful garlicky, lemony flavours and the juices are amazing – with or without cream. A Sunday treat.

1 Preheat the oven to 200°C/180°C Fan/Gas 6. Separate the head of garlic into cloves. Don't peel them but just prick them all with a sharp knife and set aside.

2 Heat the oil in a large casserole dish. Add the bacon, shallots or onions and the mushrooms and fry them gently over a medium heat until they're all starting to soften and colour around the edges. Add most of the garlic cloves and 1 sprig of thyme, then sprinkle over the lemon zest.

3 Season the inside of the chicken cavity and pop in the other sprig of thyme and the rest of the garlic cloves. Spread the butter over the skin on the top of the chicken and season with salt and pepper.

4 Push the vegetables to the edges of the casserole dish and put the chicken in the centre. Pour in the stock around the sides.

5 Place the casserole dish on the hob and bring the stock to the boil, then put the lid on the dish and put it in the oven. Cook for 50 minutes, remove the lid and cook for another 20 minutes – the chicken skin should brown and crisp up in this time.

6 Check that the chicken is done – the juices should run clear in the thickest part of the leg when pierced with a skewer and the legs should feel loose if you pull them. If the chicken isn't quite done, put it back in the oven for another 5–10 minutes. When the chicken is cooked, transfer it to a serving platter, then remove the vegetables with a slotted spoon and add them to the platter with the chicken. Cover with foil to keep everything warm.

7 Squeeze the flesh out of the garlic cloves into the cooking liquid in the casserole dish and discard the skins. Simmer the liquid until it has reduced – the garlic will make it lovely and creamy but if you want it thicker still, add the double cream.

8 Taste the gravy and add a squeeze of lemon juice if you think it needs it. Pour the gravy into a warm jug or gravy boat and serve it with the chicken and vegetables. Sprinkle the veg with a handful of parsley before taking them to the table. This is lovely with some brown rice to soak up the juices.

Serves 4

1 head of garlic
1 tbsp olive oil
6 streaky bacon rashers, chopped
400g shallots or small onions, peeled
250g button mushrooms, wiped clean and left whole
2 large sprigs of thyme
grated zest of 1 lemon
generous slice of butter
1 x 1.2–1.5kg chicken
300ml chicken stock (see page 210)
100ml double cream (optional)
salt and black pepper

To serve
squeeze of lemon juice
handful of parsley leaves, roughly chopped

Chicken and roast vegetable tray bake

Another wonderful one-pot, this is really easy, tastes good and the kids like it, so it's a great dish for a family supper. And there's no need to brown the chicken first – it browns beautifully in the oven.

1 Preheat the oven to 200°C/180°C Fan/Gas 6.

2 Bring a saucepan of water to the boil and add the potatoes. Bring the water back to the boil and cook the potatoes for 2 minutes to parboil them, then drain them thoroughly.

3 Put all the vegetables, including the potatoes, in a large roasting tin. Whisk together the olive oil, paprika and lemon juice, then drizzle half this mixture over the vegetables. Pour the rest over the chicken and rub it in, then place the chicken on top of the vegetables. Sprinkle over the herbs and season everything with salt and pepper.

4 Cover the roasting tin with foil and put it in the oven for half an hour. At the end of this time, have a quick look at the vegetables – they should feel tender when pierced with a knife.

5 Remove the foil and add the cherry tomatoes, then put the tin back in the oven, uncovered, for another 15–20 minutes, until the chicken is well browned and cooked through. Serve sprinkled with black olives and basil leaves.

Serves 4

200g new potatoes, sliced
1 large aubergine, cut into thick rounds
1 red pepper, deseeded and cut into thick strips
1 red onion, cut into wedges
3 tbsp olive oil
1 tsp sweet smoked paprika
juice of ½ lemon
8 chicken thighs or 8 chicken legs, bone in and skin on
1 tsp dried herbes de Provence
16 cherry tomatoes, left whole
handful of black olives, pitted
large handful of basil leaves
salt and black pepper

Cassoulet

My heart is in France and this French classic is a favourite winter warmer in our household. Here's my quick version, using ordinary duck breasts instead of the traditional duck confit (preserved duck). Lovely with greens and bacon (see page 136).

1 Preheat the oven to 200°C/180°C Fan/Gas 6.

2 Heat a large heavy-based casserole dish on the hob and add the duck breasts, skin-side down. Fry them until the skin is a deep brown and much of the fat has come out. Transfer the duck breasts to a roasting dish and put them in the oven for 20 minutes.

3 Fry the sausages in the duck fat in the casserole dish. When the sausages are well browned all over, remove them from the dish and set aside, then drain off most of the fat. Add the bacon and onion and fry until the bacon is crisp and brown. Add the garlic and cook for another couple of minutes.

4 Tip the beans into the casserole dish and add the sausages and the bouquet garni, then season with salt and pepper. Add the tomatoes, then pour in enough water to just cover the beans.

5 Remove the duck breasts from the oven, cut them into slices and add them to the cassoulet. Make sure the sausages and duck meat are well pushed down into the beans.

6 Put the cassoulet in the oven, uncovered, and cook for 45–60 minutes, until the liquid has reduced and a crust has developed. Serve with some green vegetables.

Serves 4

2 duck breasts
4 Toulouse sausages
100g smoked bacon, cut into thin strips
1 onion, thickly sliced
6 garlic cloves, finely sliced
3 x 400g cans of cannellini beans
bouquet garni (see below)
2 ripe tomatoes, puréed in a food processor
salt and black pepper

Bouquet garni
large sprig of thyme
2 large sprigs of parsley
2 bay leaves

Davina's tip
A bouquet garni is just a little bundle of herbs for flavouring dishes, French style. The herbs can vary according to the dish, but a simple one is right for this. Tie the herbs together with a piece of cooking string and don't forget to remove them before serving.

Pork, bean and sweet potato chilli

I've realised that I tend to get stuck in a rut with recipes and make the same things over and over. This variation on chilli using pork mince is amazing and is a nice change from the regular beef version. Chipotle paste is great and you can find it in most supermarkets.

1 Heat the oil in a large saucepan or casserole dish and add the onion and red pepper. Fry them gently over a low to medium heat for several minutes until they're just starting to soften, then add the garlic and cook for another minute.

2 Add the pork mince and stir until it's all well browned. Sprinkle in the cumin, oregano and chipotle paste, then tip in the beans and chopped tomatoes.

3 Pour 400ml of water into the pan, then add the diced sweet potatoes and push them well into the chilli.

4 Bring the mixture to the boil, then turn the heat down to a simmer and cover the pan. Simmer the chilli for half an hour, then take the lid off the pan and simmer for another 15 minutes to reduce the sauce. Taste and check the seasoning.

5 Serve with garnishes such as brown basmati rice, grated cheese, diced avocado, soured cream, handfuls of chopped fresh coriander and lime wedges – as many of these as you like.

- -

Davina's tips

This is fantastic made in an Aga if you have one. I cook mine in the simmering oven for three hours and it is SO good.

PS: Don't be put off by the porky smell while this is cooking. It tastes really yummy.

PPS: You don't even need rice if you don't fancy it. Great with just the avocado, cheese and soured cream.

PPPS: You're lovely!

Serves 4

2 tbsp olive oil
1 large onion, chopped
1 red pepper, chopped
2 garlic cloves, finely chopped
500g pork mince
2 tsp cumin powder
1 tsp dried oregano
1 tsp chipotle paste or other hot
    sauce (to taste)
400g can of beans (pinto,
    black-eyed peas, black),
    drained and rinsed
400g can of chopped tomatoes
250g sweet potatoes (1 large or
    2 small), peeled and cut into
    large dice
salt and black pepper

Ham hock with vegetables

I was a bit frightened by the idea of cooking ham hock at first, but I tried it, it's easy and I love it. This makes an excellent one-pot supper as it is, but you could also serve the ham with mashed potatoes. Be sure to save the leftover cooking liquid for making ham and split pea soup (see page 65).

1 Put the ham hock in a deep saucepan or stockpot and cover it with water. Bring the water to the boil and simmer for 1 minute, then drain, discarding the water – this is important for getting rid of excess saltiness so don't be tempted to skip this step! Rinse the ham thoroughly to remove any starchy foam that might be sticking to it. Put it back in the saucepan and cover with fresh water.

2 Add the onion, bay leaves and peppercorns to the pan. Bring the water to the boil, then turn down the heat to a gentle to medium simmer and cover the pan with a lid. Cook the ham for an hour to an hour and a half, depending on the weight.

3 Remove the ham from the liquid. When it's cool enough to handle, strip away the skin, fat and bone, then pull the meat into large chunks.

4 Measure the cooking liquid and pour 500ml of it back into the saucepan – keep the rest for making soup. Add the vegetables, apples and sage, to the pan and simmer for 15–20 minutes, covered, until the veg are tender. Season with black pepper. Serve the ham hot with the vegetables but any leftover meat will be great cold.

Serves 4

1 ham hock, 1–1.5kg in weight
1 onion, studded with 2 cloves
2 bay leaves
1 tsp peppercorns
2 large carrots, cut into chunks
  on the diagonal
2 leeks, cut into thick rounds
200g swede, peeled and cut
  into chunks
1 large floury potato, peeled
  and diced
¼ green cabbage, shredded
2 eating apples (such as Cox),
  peeled, cored and cut into
  wedges
1 tsp dried sage
black pepper

Slow-roast Moroccan lamb

This is amazing. The meat is marinated first and cooked for ages until it falls meltingly off the bone. I love it. I have to admit I was a bit dubious about the idea of adding the tomatoes but it works brilliantly I promise you. The tomatoes cook down into a gorgeously sticky sauce that's just right with the spice-crusted lamb. Ras-el-hanout is a spice mix that's available in most supermarkets and includes more than 20 different spices such as cardamom, nutmeg, cinnamon and cloves as well as rosebuds. No wonder it tastes so good.

1 Cut slits all over the lamb with the tip of a sharp knife. Mix the ras-el-hanout with the oil, garlic, lemon juice, saffron, if using, and salt and black pepper. Rub this all over the lamb, top and bottom, then leave the meat to marinate for at least a couple of hours. You can wrap it in foil and leave it in the fridge overnight if you prefer.

2 Preheat the oven to 240°C/220°C Fan/Gas 9. Spread the slices of onion over the base of a roasting tin and put the lamb on top of them. Pour the stock around the lamb and season with salt and pepper.

3 Roast the meat at the high temperature for 30 minutes to get a good crust, then reduce the heat to 150°C/130°C Fan/Gas 2. Roast the lamb for another 3–4 hours, depending on the weight of your joint and add the tomatoes after the first 2 hours. When it's ready, the meat should be very tender and falling off the bone.

4 Remove the lamb from the oven, cover with foil and leave to rest for 20 minutes. Reheat the pan juices, stir in the herbs and serve with the meat. Some barley couscous goes well with this and perhaps some green vegetables, such as my green beans with almonds and lemon zest, and greens with bacon and garlic, both on page 136. No need for carving – you can just pull the meat apart.

Serves 4–6

1 shoulder of lamb, on the bone
2 tbsp ras-el-hanout
2 tbsp olive oil
3 garlic cloves, crushed
juice of 1 lemon
pinch of saffron threads (optional)
1 large onion, thickly sliced
500ml chicken stock (see page 210)
400g can of chopped tomatoes
handfuls of mint, parsley and/or
    coriander, to serve
salt and black pepper

Shepherd's pie

We always joke about the difference between shepherd's pie and cottage pie in our house. It's easy – shepherds have sheep! I used to add Worcestershire sauce to my shepherd's pie but it contains sugar so no more of that. Some of my home-made ketchup adds a nice touch of sweetness, though, and you can also add a dash of wine if you like (and you don't mind the sugar). The sweet potato topping is awesome and makes a welcome change from regular mash.

1 Heat the oil in a large casserole dish or saucepan. Add half the lamb and brown it thoroughly, allowing a crust to develop on the underside before turning it over. Remove the meat and set it aside, then add the remaining lamb and brown it in the same way. Put all the lamb back in the pan.

2 Add the onion, carrots, celery and celeriac or swede to the pan and cook for 10 minutes over a medium heat until the vegetables have softened. Add the garlic, cinnamon and rosemary and stir to combine, then add the tomatoes and stock and season with salt and pepper. Bring everything to the boil, then turn down the heat and cover the pan with a lid. Simmer gently for about 45 minutes, checking regularly to make sure the mixture isn't getting too dry. If necessary, add a little more stock or water.

3 While the meat is cooking, you can make the sweet potato mash. Preheat the oven to 200°C/180°C Fan/Gas 6. Put the sweet potatoes on a baking tray and bake them for 45 minutes or so until soft. Remove them from the oven but leave the oven on. As soon as the sweet potatoes are cool enough to handle, split them open and scoop the flesh out into a bowl. Add the crème fraiche, season with salt and black pepper and mash thoroughly.

4 To assemble, put the meat mixture in an ovenproof serving dish. Spoon the sweet potato mash on top, spreading it out evenly and making sure that none of the meat bleeds through, then fork up the mash slightly for a rougher finish. Dot with a few small knobs of butter. Bake the pie in the hot oven for about 40–45 minutes.

Serves 6

1 tbsp olive oil
600g minced lamb
1 onion, finely chopped
2 carrots, diced
2 celery sticks, diced
100g celeriac or swede, finely diced
2 garlic cloves, finely chopped
¼ tsp cinnamon
a few rosemary leaves, finely chopped
400g can of chopped tomatoes
300ml lamb or chicken stock
salt and black pepper

Topping

2–3 sweet potatoes (about 1kg in weight)
2 tbsp crème fraiche
a few knobs of butter, for dotting on top

Beef stir-fry

This is both fabulously healthy and sustaining. It does look like quite a lot of ingredients I know, but there's nothing difficult and I like to do my TV chef act and quietly chop and slice until everything is ready in little bowls. Then it cooks in minutes and you have a feast. There are so many veg in this I don't think you need noodles, but you could add a little chilli if you like a bit of heat.

1 Bring a pan of water to the boil, add the beans and cook them briefly. Drain and refresh the beans under cold water to stop them cooking, then set them aside.

2 Heat a tablespoon of the oil in a large wok. When it's smoking, add the beef and stir-fry it very quickly until browned. You might need to do this in a couple of batches as it is important not to overcrowd the pan or the beef will stew and not brown. Remove the beef from the wok and set it aside.

3 Add the rest of the oil to the wok and again, when it's smoking, add the onion, garlic and ginger. Stir-fry for a minute only, then sprinkle in the Chinese five-spice. Add all the vegetables, except the Chinese greens, then continue to fry for another 2–3 minutes.

4 Pour in the soy sauce along with 2 tablespoons of water and season with salt and pepper. Lay the greens on top and leave them to steam for a couple of minutes until wilted – this 'covering' will help the vegetables soften slightly too.

5 Put the slices of beef back in the wok and mix with everything else to heat them through. Drizzle over the sesame oil and serve at once.

- -

Davina's tip
My kids don't like shiitake mushrooms, so if I'm making this for a family meal I use ordinary button ones and they're fine.

Serves 4

100g green beans, trimmed
2 tbsp vegetable oil
500g beef steak (rump or sirloin) trimmed and cut into thin slices
1 onion, cut into thin wedges
2 garlic cloves, finely chopped
10g fresh root ginger, peeled and finely chopped
1 tsp Chinese five-spice powder
1 large head of broccoli, broken into small florets, then halved
1 large carrot, cut into thin batons
1 red pepper, cut into slices lengthways
200g shiitake mushrooms, thickly sliced
2 tbsp soy sauce
a bag of Chinese greens (pak choi or similar)
1 tsp sesame oil
salt and black pepper

Burgers

When it comes to burgers, make your own. They always taste better. These are great with my ketchup and/or mayo (see pages 210–212) and served with wholemeal buns, salad and perhaps a slice or two of bacon. You can also use the mixture to make sliders or meatballs. If you make meatballs, serve them with spelt pasta and tomato sauce.

1 Put the meat in a bowl and season it with salt and pepper. Heat the olive oil in a frying pan, add the onion and fry it until soft. Add the garlic and cook for another minute.

2 Let the onion and garlic cool slightly, then add them to the meat, along with all the other ingredients. Mix thoroughly the best way to do this is with your hands. Put the mixture in the fridge for half an hour to firm up a bit.

3 Divide the mixture, according to how you want to serve it. For burgers, shape the mixture into 6 portions. For sliders, divide into about 8. To make meatballs, divide into 20 balls about the size of a golfball. Preheat the oven to 220°C/200°C Fan/Gas 7.

4 Bake the burgers, sliders or meatballs in the oven for about 15 minutes. They are all about the same thickness so the timing works for all. For cheeseburgers, add slices of cheese on top of each burger for the last 2 minutes of the cooking time.

- -

Davina's tip
These freeze really well so cook up a batch to stash away, ready to serve for super-quick suppers.

Makes 6 burgers, 8 sliders or 20 meatballs

500g mince (beef, lamb or a combination of beef and pork)
1 tbsp olive oil
1 onion, finely chopped
1 garlic clove, finely chopped
1 egg
25ml milk, cream or 25g cream cheese
½ tsp dried herbs
100g wholemeal breadcrumbs
1 tbsp freshly chopped parsley
salt and black pepper

Ragù sauce

Ragù is the Italian name for the meat sauce usually served with spaghetti. It's wonderful, everyone loves it and it can be used in all sorts of dishes, such as shepherd's pie, as well as with spelt or wholewheat pasta. It needs to cook for ages, but this really does make a difference to the flavour.

1 Heat a tablespoon of the olive oil in a large saucepan and start browning the meat. It's best to do this in 3 or 4 batches, as if you add all the meat at once, it will boil rather than fry and you won't get any caramelisation. Remove each batch of meat once it is well browned and set it aside.

2 Add the remaining olive oil to the saucepan, then fry the onion until it's starting to soften – this should take about 5 minutes. Add the garlic, herbs and bay leaf, then put the meat back into the pan.

3 Pour the red wine into the pan and bring it to the boil. When it has reduced by at least half, add 500ml of stock, the tomatoes and tomato paste and season with salt and black pepper. Bring it all back to the boil, then cover the pan and turn down the heat.

4 Simmer the ragù gently for an hour, then take the lid off the pan and continue to cook for another 30 minutes to 1 hour until the sauce has reduced down. Add more stock if you need and stir regularly to make sure the sauce doesn't catch on the bottom of the pan.

5 Serve with wholewheat or spelt pasta.

Davina's tip
OMG, this is one of my kids' very favourites – it is delish. Make a big batch of the sauce and freeze it in portions for quick suppers.

Serves 4–6

2 tbsp olive oil
500g lean beef mince
500g pork mince
1 onion, finely chopped
3 garlic cloves, finely chopped
1 tsp dried oregano or mixed
    dried herbs
1 bay leaf
200ml red wine
500–800ml beef stock
400g can of chopped tomatoes,
    puréed
1 tbsp tomato paste
salt and black pepper

Davina's favourites

5 Super Sides

"Did you know my roast potatoes are the best in the world? Well now you do. And I often leave the skins on for extra fibre."

Green beans with almonds and lemon zest

This goes brilliantly with meat or fish and you can cook runner beans in the same way.

1 Pinch the tops off the beans but leave their thin tails in place. Bring a saucepan of water to the boil. Drop in the beans and simmer them for about 5 minutes until they are just tender and still a vibrant green. Drain thoroughly.

2 Heat a frying pan over a medium heat. Add the almonds and dry-fry them for a minute, shaking regularly, until they're just starting to toast.

3 Add the olive oil and butter to the pan. When the butter has melted, add the green beans, lemon zest and seasoning. Turn everything over so the beans are well coated and serve immediately.

Serves 4

200g fine green beans
2 tbsp flaked almonds
1 tbsp olive oil
1 knob of butter
grated zest of ½ lemon
salt and black pepper

Greens with bacon and garlic

Bacon is a perfect partner for greens. Use any type – spring greens, savoy cabbage, kale, cavolo nero and chard all work well.

1 Wash the greens and discard any very tough stems. Don't drain them too well – it helps if the leaves are still holding on to some water. Shred the greens quite finely into strips about 1cm wide.

2 Heat the olive oil in a large lidded saucepan. Add the bacon and fry until it's crisp and brown and it has released some fat. Add the chopped garlic and stir for another minute.

3 Add the greens to the pan. Don't worry if they crowd the saucepan – they will soon wilt down. Stir until they start to collapse, turning them over until they are well coated with the oil and bacon. Season with salt and black pepper.

4 Add 100ml water to the pan and put the lid on. Cook for a few minutes, until the greens have wilted but still have some bite to them. Drain them lightly, so you don't lose all the lovely juices, then serve.

Serves 4

large bag of greens
1 tbsp olive oil
100g smoked bacon, chopped
2 garlic cloves, finely chopped
salt and black pepper

Home-made baked beans

These are great in their own right – I'm not trying to make something that tastes like canned beans. Eat them on their own, with sausages or just a salad on the side. Excellent.

1 Heat the olive oil in a large saucepan. Add the chopped onion and cook over a medium heat for several minutes until it's softened and starting to caramelise.

2 Add the bacon to the pan and fry until crisp, then add the tomatoes, paprika and a teaspoon of maple syrup. Season well with salt and black pepper. Simmer for about 20 minutes until the tomatoes have reduced down into a thick sauce, then taste and add more seasoning and maple syrup if you think it necessary.

3 Purée the sauce – there'll be some flecks of bacon in it but that's fine. Add the beans, then simmer for a few minutes to warm them through before serving.

Serves 4

2 tbsp olive oil
1 large onion, finely chopped
100g smoked bacon, chopped
400g can of chopped tomatoes
1 tsp sweet smoked paprika
1–2 tsp maple syrup, to taste
2 x 400g cans of haricot or
    cannellini beans, drained
    and rinsed
salt and black pepper

Cauliflower cheese

I make my cheese sauce with wholemeal spelt flour now, which makes it look slightly speckly but it tastes absolutely delicious.

1 Preheat the oven to 220°C/200°C Fan/Gas 7.

2 Bring a large saucepan of water to the boil. Add the cauliflower florets and cook for 3-4 minutes – you don't want them too soft and they should still have some bite to them. Drain and refresh the cauliflower under cold water.

3 To make the cheese sauce, melt the butter in a saucepan. Add the flour and stir thoroughly for a couple of minutes to cook the flour. This is important, as the flour can taste raw if not toasted in this way first. Gradually add the milk, about 100ml at a time, stirring constantly between each addition, until it is all incorporated and you have a smooth if runny sauce.

4 Turn up the heat slightly and continue to stir the sauce until it comes to the boil and thickens. Season with salt and pepper. Add 75g of the grated cheese and stir until it has melted into the sauce.

5 Put the cauliflower in an ovenproof dish and pour the sauce over it. Arrange the slices of tomato on top. Mix the remaining cheese with the breadcrumbs, if using, and sprinkle it over the tomatoes. Put the dish in the oven and bake for 15–20 minutes until the cheese is golden brown and bubbling.

Serves 4

1 large cauliflower, broken into florets
50g butter
50g wholemeal spelt flour
500ml whole milk
100g Cheddar cheese (or similar hard cheese), grated
2 or 3 tomatoes, sliced
25g wholemeal breadcrumbs (optional)
salt and black pepper

Vegetable purées

I'm always looking for good side dishes and these are all so easy and so versatile. I love them. Great for soaking up delicious juices.

Cannellini bean purée

1 Put the milk and beans in a saucepan and season with salt and black pepper. Cover and warm the beans through for a few minutes.

2 Heat the butter gently in a frying pan. When it's melted and foaming, add the sage and cook it for a minute, then add the butter and sage to the beans and milk. Tip it all into a blender or food processor and puree, then put it back into the pan to keep warm until ready to serve.

All serve 4

100ml whole milk
2 x 400g cans of cannellini
  beans, drained and rinsed
15g butter
1 tsp dried sage
salt and black pepper

Carrot and swede purée

1 Put the carrots and swede in a saucepan and cover with cold water. Bring to the boil, then turn the heat down and simmer the vegetables for about 15 minutes until they're tender. Drain them thoroughly in a colander, then cover with a tea towel for a few minutes so that they really dry out.

2 While the vegetables are still in the colander, press down on the swede very gently to release a bit more water, then tip everything into a bowl. Roughly mash the veg with a fork, then season with salt and black pepper and stir in the butter. The mix won't be that smooth – it's more of a crush than a silky purée.

4 medium carrots (about 300g),
  sliced
1 small swede (about 300g), diced
15g butter
salt and black pepper

Pea purée

1 Put the peas in a saucepan with the butter and dried mint. Add 50ml of water and season with salt and pepper. Put a lid on the pan and simmer the peas for about 5 minutes until they are just tender.

2 Tip the contents of the saucepan into a blender or food processor, add the crème fraiche and blitz to a rough purée. Put the purée back in the pan to keep warm until ready to serve.

400g peas, fresh or frozen
15g butter
½ tsp dried mint
1 tbsp crème fraiche
salt and black pepper

Creamy vegetable gratin

This had me at creamy. Enjoy. It's fine to leave the skin on the potatoes if they're in good condition, but I like to peel the other veg.

1 Preheat the oven to 200°C/180°C Fan/Gas 6. Rub the cut garlic clove over the inside of a shallow 1-litre ovenproof dish and then grease the dish with butter.

2 Slice all the vegetables as thinly as you can. Arrange them in layers in the dish, starting and finishing with layers of potato. Season each layer as you go.

3 Mix together the milk and double cream and pour them over the vegetables. Sprinkle with grated cheese.

4 Bake the gratin in the oven for about 45 minutes, until the vegetables are tender when you test them with a knife and the cheese has melted and browned.

Serves 4

1 garlic clove, cut in half
butter, for greasing
3 large potatoes (about 600g)
3 carrots
½ a small swede (about 150g)
¼ pumpkin or butternut squash
  (about 200g)
½ small onion, finely sliced
300ml whole milk
300ml double cream
50g Gruyère or Cheddar cheese,
  grated
salt and black pepper

Roast potatoes

My roast potatoes are the best in the world – maybe in my head! – and it's all about the parboiling. You have to get it just right so you can fluff the potatoes up nicely without them falling apart. And make sure the fat is really, really hot. If the potatoes are in good condition, leave them unpeeled for the extra fibre and nutrients.

1 Preheat the oven to 200°C/180°C Fan/Gas 6. Put the fat or oil in a large roasting tin and place it in the oven to heat up.

2 Put the potatoes in a large saucepan and cover them with water. Bring them to the boil and cook them for 2 minutes. Drain thoroughly, tip the potatoes back in the pan and shake them furiously, holding the lid of the pan in place.

3 Carefully remove the tin of hot fat or oil from the oven – make sure it's really hot. Add the potatoes, holding the tin away from you as you do this as the fat is likely to splatter. Roast the potatoes for 45–50 minutes until crisp and brown on the outside, fluffy on the inside. Serve immediately. Never keep roast potatoes waiting.

Serves 4

1kg floury potatoes (Maris Pipers or King Edwards are good), cut into chunks
50g duck/goose fat or olive oil

Smashed new potatoes

These are simplicity itself to do and almost like mini jacket potatoes. Lovely topped with some sea salt and butter.

1 Preheat the oven to 200°C/180°C Fan/Gas 6. Put the new potatoes in a large saucepan, cover them with water and bring to the boil. Simmer the potatoes for 8–10 minutes, until they are almost cooked through, then drain and dry them as thoroughly as you can.

2 Spread the potatoes out in a roasting tin. Squash each potato very slightly on the sides so it breaks open at the top. Drizzle over some olive oil – a tablespoon should be enough – then season with sea salt.

3 Roast the potatoes in the oven for about 30 minutes. Pile them into a large serving dish and dot with butter.

Serves 4

1kg small new potatoes
drizzle of olive oil
sea salt
25g butter

Potato, root vegetable and garlic mash

You can partner potatoes with any root veg, such as parsnips, Jerusalem artichokes or swede, but I particularly like celeriac for flavour. I like to leave the skin on potatoes whenever possible, but somehow skin-flecked mash doesn't seem quite right so I always peel them for this. Lots of garlic adds zing to a mash.

1 Put the potatoes in a large saucepan, cover them with water and bring them to the boil. Cut the celeriac into chunks and add them and the garlic cloves to the pan. Simmer for about 15 minutes until tender.

2 Drain, then mash everything well, including the garlic. Season with salt and pepper and stir in the crème fraiche.

Serves 4

500g floury potatoes (Maris Pipers or King Edwards are good), peeled and cut into chunks
500g celeriac, peeled
½ head of garlic cloves, peeled
2 tbsp crème fraiche
salt and black pepper

Sweet potato fries

If the skins on your sweet potatoes are in good condition, keep them on. Otherwise peel them. If you need to wash the potatoes, before or after peeling, make sure you dry them thoroughly before coating them in oil. These are lovely with the fish patties on page 100.

1 Preheat the oven to 200°C/180°C Fan/Gas 6. Line a large baking tray with greaseproof paper.

2 Cut the sweet potatoes into slim chips – ½–1cm wide. Put them in a bowl and drizzle over the olive oil, then toss the potatoes in the oil to make sure they are thoroughly coated. Sprinkle with salt, black pepper and smoked paprika, if using.

3 Spread the fries over the baking tray, then put them in the oven and bake for 30–35 minutes until they're crisp and brown round the edges. Check the fries from time to time and turn them over once or twice.

Serves 4

800g sweet potatoes (about 5 or 6)
2 tbsp olive oil
1 tsp sweet smoked paprika (optional)
salt and black pepper

Roast root vegetables

Vegetables like carrots and parsnips are naturally sweet, but I do like to drizzle them with a bit of honey sometimes for a special treat. It does something rather amazing. You could also vary this recipe by adding other lovely flavours such as lemon zest or cumin to the veg.

1 Preheat the oven to 200°C/180°C Fan/Gas 6.

2 Peel all the vegetables and trim off their tops. Cut the carrots and parsnips lengthways into batons. If the carrots are very long, cut the batons in half. Cut each beetroot into 8 wedges. Cut the celeriac into cubes of 3–4cm.

3 Put the vegetables in a large roasting tin. Tuck in the sprigs of thyme, then drizzle over the olive oil. Mix well, so everything has an even coating of oil, then make sure all the vegetables are evenly spread out. Season with salt and black pepper.

4 Roast the vegetables for about an hour, turning them over once or twice, until they're all tender and nicely browned round the edges and in patches.

5 If using honey, drizzle it over the veggies after the first 45 minutes, then continue to cook for another 15 minutes.

Serves 4

4 carrots (about 300g)
2–4 parsnips, depending on size (about 300g)
3 medium beetroots (about 300g)
½ medium celeriac (about 300g)
a few sprigs of thyme
2 tbsp olive oil
1 tbsp honey (optional)
salt and black pepper

Davina's favourites

6 Life-Saving Snacks

"Mmmm . . . power balls, veggie crisps. We all need a little something from time to time."

Vegetable crisps

Love these and they make the perfect snack to stave off hunger pangs when it seems a long time until supper. You can use any root vegetables, but parsnips, beetroots and sweet potatoes are especially good. You can also add extra flavours if you like, such as chilli and spices.

1 Preheat the oven to 160°/140°C Fan/Gas 3.

2 Peel the vegetables if necessary, but you can leave them unpeeled if the skins are good. Slice them as thinly as you can. You can do this with a mandolin, or use a vegetable peeler instead and try to get the strips as wide and as thin (no more than 1mm) as you can.

3 Make sure the vegetables are bone dry, then put them in a large bowl. Drizzle over the oil and, using your hands, fold it into the vegetables, making sure everything is evenly coated.

4 Arrange the vegetables in a single layer on as many baking trays as necessary. I use 3, but you may have to cook your crisps in a few batches, depending on how many baking trays you have. Put the veg in the oven and bake until they're crisp and browned. This should take 25–30 minutes, but keep a close eye on them to make sure they are not going too dark.

5 Remove the crisps from the oven and when they're cool, toss them with some sea salt. Store the crisps in an airtight container to keep them fresh – although they don't last long when I'm around!

½–1 sweet potato, depending on size
1 fat parsnip
1 medium beetroot
1 tbsp vegetable oil
sea salt

Bruschetta

These are basically lovely things on toast. I make bruschetta all the time and it's always popular. You can experiment with different toppings, but here are a couple of my favourites and each one makes enough for 4 small bruschettas. Taleggio is a semi-soft Italian cheese that melts beautifully but if you don't have any, use any other cheese that melts well, such as Gruyère. Blue cheese is good too.

1 Toast the slices of bread. Rub one side of each slice with the cut garlic, then drizzle with a little olive oil.

2 To make the mushroom topping, preheat the grill to its highest setting. Put the olive oil and butter in a frying pan. When the butter starts to foam, add the mushrooms, garlic and thyme and season with salt and black pepper. Cook over a high heat, stirring regularly, until the mushrooms have cooked through and browned.

3 Divide the mushrooms between the slices of bread and put the cheese on top. Put the bruschetta under the grill until the cheese has melted and is bubbling.

4 To make the broad bean, ham and ricotta topping, bring a saucepan of water to the boil and add the broad beans. Cook them for 4 minutes, then drain. Slip the greyish skin off each bean and discard.

5 Heat a tablespoon of oil in a frying pan. Add the ham and fry it briefly until brown, then add the broad beans and season with salt and black pepper.

6 Spread a tablespoon of ricotta over each slice of toast. Divide the broad bean and ham mix between the bruschetta. Finish with a squeeze of lemon juice and a drizzle of olive oil, then sprinkle with basil leaves before serving.

Serves 4

4 slices of good sourdough or other firm wholemeal bread
1 garlic clove, halved lengthways
olive oil

Mushroom and taleggio topping

1 tbsp olive oil
10g butter
400g portobellini or button mushrooms, sliced
1 garlic clove, chopped
a few sprigs of thyme
4 slices of taleggio cheese
salt and black pepper

Broad bean, ham and ricotta topping

200g broad beans (fresh or frozen)
1 tbsp olive oil, plus more for drizzling
2 slices of Parma ham, pulled into small pieces
4 tbsp fresh ricotta
a squeeze of lemon juice
a few torn basil leaves
salt and black pepper

Dips

It's comforting to have a dip in the fridge to enjoy with some sticks of raw veg, wholemeal crispbreads or the vegetable crisps on page 154. I've found it hard to make a hummus that tastes as good as shop-bought – you get used to that texture somehow – but I think this is it. I love all of these.

Hummus

1 Put the chickpeas, tahini, cumin, if using, and salt in a food processor. Add the juice of 1 lemon and pulse, adding tablespoons of water until you have a smooth, creamy paste. Taste, then add more lemon juice if you think the mixture needs it.

2 Spoon the hummus into a container or serving dish and top with a generous drizzle of olive oil and a sprinkling of cayenne.

400g can of chickpeas, drained and rinsed
2 tbsp tahini
a pinch of ground cumin (optional)
½ tsp sea salt
juice of 1½ lemons
olive oil, to serve
a pinch of cayenne, to serve

Roast beetroot dip

1 Preheat the oven to 180°C/160°C Fan/Gas 4. Wash the beetroots and dry them with kitchen towel. Rub the beetroot with a tablespoon of the oil, place them in a roasting tin and sprinkle with sea salt.

2 Cover the tin with foil and roast the beetroots in the oven for 45–60 minutes, depending on their size. The beetroots are done when the tip of a knife pierces through to the centre very easily.

3 Remove the beetroots from the oven and when they're cool enough to handle, rub off the skins. Chop the beetroots roughly, then put them in a blender with another tablespoon of olive oil, the garlic, cumin and Greek yoghurt and blitz until smooth. Taste and season with black pepper and salt if necessary and add a squeeze of lemon juice.

6 small beetroots or 3 medium-large (about 300g in all)
2 tbsp olive oil
1 garlic clove, finely chopped
1 tsp cumin
2 tbsp Greek yoghurt
squeeze of lemon juice
sea salt and black pepper

Guacamole

1 Peel the avocados and remove the stones. Cut the flesh into bite-sized pieces, then mash with a fork. Leave a few pieces whole, so you get a mixture of textures.

2 Add the onion, finely chopped tomato, coriander and the chilli, if using. Pour over the lime juice and season well with salt and pepper. Mix everything together and chill until ready to serve.

2 large ripe avocados
½ red onion, very finely chopped
1 tomato, deseeded and chopped
small bunch coriander, chopped
1 mild red chilli, finely chopped (optional)
juice of 1 lime
salt and black pepper

Pitta pizzas

This is a brilliant idea and ridiculously simple to do. These are really store cupboard pizzas, designed to be made with whatever you have in your fridge and cupboards, and it's fun for everyone to put together their own.

1 Preheat the oven to its highest setting.

2 Mix together all the sauce ingredients. Put the pitta bases on a baking tray and divide the sauce between them – you should have at least a generously heaped tablespoon per pitta base. Then cover the sauce with cheese – there should be plenty if sliced thinly enough.

3 Top with whatever you like from the list. You'll probably come up with lots of other ideas too. You can make 4 completely different pizzas if necessary and they will all cook in the same time. Drizzle your pizzas with olive oil – about 2 teaspoons per pitta.

4 Put the pizzas in the oven and bake them for 5–10 minutes, watching them carefully to make sure they don't burn. Serve immediately.

Serves 4

2 wholewheat pitta breads, each
   split into 2 thin bases

Sauce
2 tbsp tomato purée
4 tbsp canned tomatoes, very
   finely chopped
2 garlic cloves
½ tsp dried oregano
large handful of basil, finely
   chopped

Cheese
1 x 150g mozzarella, finely sliced

Toppings
thinly sliced mushrooms
thinly sliced red onions
roast peppers or aubergines
a few olives and capers
canned anchovies, drained
canned tuna, drained
a few slices of Parma ham
sliced artichokes in oil
drizzle of olive oil, to finish

Power balls

When I'm going out on a big cycle ride I like to stash some of these in my bike pouch for when the urge to snack hits. Anything I've tried before has been loaded with sugar but these are just right. Great for before or after a workout too – I don't want sugary snacks any more. You can use any type of nut butter but peanut can be overpowering and is often salted. Try cashew, almond or hazelnut butter or there is a nice three-nut one.

1 Put the nut butter and honey in a saucepan and stir them over a low heat until they have melted together.

2 Remove the pan from the heat and stir in the cocoa, coconut (or coconut and oatmeal) and the sesame seeds. Mix very thoroughly until everything has come together in a firm but sticky mixture. Allow this to cool completely, then chill in the fridge for about 10 minutes to make rolling easier.

3 Roll the mixture into walnut-sized balls, then roll each one in a coating of your choice. Store them in the fridge in an airtight container.

100g crunchy nut butter
100g honey
25g cocoa powder
100g desiccated coconut OR
   50g desiccated coconut and
   50g oatmeal
25g sesame seeds
extra desiccated coconut, cocoa,
   or sesame seeds, for rolling

Fruit leather

I know this sounds a bit of a faff but it's fun to do and it contains all the fibre of the fruit so is healthier than fruit juice. Great for the kids to snack on and you can use any combination of fruits. You don't have to peel apples and pears but the fruit will need puréeing before sieving.

1 Preheat the oven to its lowest setting – usually about 50°C. Line a baking sheet with greaseproof paper and oil it very lightly.

2 Dice the apples or pears and put them in a saucepan with 50ml of water and the lemon juice. Cover and simmer the fruit gently until very soft. The time this takes will vary depending on how firm the fruit is to start with. Add the berries and simmer for a couple of minutes more until the berry juices have bled into the apples or pears.

3 Purée the fruit if you haven't peeled it, then push it through a coarse sieve. Spread the mixture as evenly as you can over the baking sheet. Don't worry if it seems very thick, as it will reduce down as the liquid evaporates from the fruit.

4 Place the tray in the oven and leave for 7–8 hours or so. When it's ready, the fruit leather will be glossy and tacky – but not sticky. Your finger will leave a print on it, but won't feel sticky when removed!

5 Remove the tray from the oven. You can then roll the fruit leather up and cut it into rounds or just into strips.

6 Fruit leather keeps indefinitely in an airtight container. Put greaseproof paper in between the layers to stop them sticking.

vegetable oil
300g eating apples or pears
juice of ½ lemon
300g berries (blueberries or
    strawberries are especially good)

Ice lollies

My children love to devour ice lollies after meals and I feel so much better about this if there's no added sugar in them. These lollies rely on the sweetness of the fruit, with a touch of maple syrup or honey. And they're made with the whole fruit, not just juice, so they contain plenty of fibre. Use any moulds you have handy, but you'll need some lolly sticks. To remove the lollies, run the moulds under a hot tap for a few seconds.

Coconut and lime ice lollies

Blitz everything together in a food processor or blender, including the zest, if using. Make sure the coconut milk is lump free. Pour the mixture into moulds, put in the sticks and freeze until solid. These lollies are quite zesty so perhaps more to the grown-ups' taste.

Each recipe makes 6 x 50ml lollies

150ml coconut milk
100ml double cream
2 tbsp maple syrup
35ml lime juice
grated lime zest (optional)

Peaches and cream ice lollies

1 Blitz the peaches with the cream or yoghurt. Taste, and add maple syrup or honey if you think it necessary. Blitz the mixture again and pour it into moulds. Put in the sticks and freeze until solid.

2 To make a version with raspberries, reduce the amount of peaches to 150g. Mash the raspberries in a bowl. Half fill the moulds with the peach mixture, then add a dessertspoon of raspberries and top up with more peach. Stir very briefly, put in the sticks and freeze until solid.

200g very ripe, peeled and stoned (or canned peaches)
100ml double cream or Greek yoghurt
1 tbsp maple syrup or honey (optional)
50g raspberries (optional)

Strawberry and blueberry ice lollies

Put all the ingredients in a blender and blitz until smooth. Pour into moulds, put in the sticks and freeze until solid.

150g strawberries
150g blueberries
juice of ½ a lime
1 tbsp maple syrup or honey

Mango lassi ice lollies

Blitz the mango and lime juice in a blender. Stir in the yoghurt, then pour into moulds, put in the sticks and freeze until solid.

1 can of mango slices, drained
juice of ½ a lime
2 tbsp Greek yoghurt

Davina's favourites

7 Puds & Bakes

"Banishing my sweet tooth is a work in progress. Now I make my sweet treats with maple syrup or honey as a step along the way."

Victoria sponge cake

Victoria sponge is usually very, very, naughty, full of white sugar, white flour – all the stuff we're not supposed to eat. When we first talked about this recipe I couldn't see how it could work with spelt flour and maple syrup. Surely it would be heavy and stodgy? How wrong I was. It's light and delicious and my daughter has now adapted the recipe to make different cakes. It's a great success and gets a big tick from me.

1 Preheat the oven to 180°C/160°C Fan/Gas 4. Grease 2 round 20cm sandwich tins and line them with baking parchment.

2 Cream the butter extra thoroughly until it's really, really soft and fluffy. This is most easily done with an electric whisk or a stand mixer. In a separate bowl, mix the spelt flour with the baking powder and whisk together until well combined.

3 Add an egg to the creamed butter, then a couple of tablespoons of the flour. Fold the flour in, then continue adding eggs and flour alternately until all the eggs have been added. Fold in the last of the flour. Mix the vanilla seeds with the maple syrup, then gently fold this into the mixture.

4 Divide the mixture between the tins and bake in the preheated oven for about 20 minutes, until the cakes are springy to touch, light brown and shrinking away from the sides of the tin. Leave them to cool in the tins until just warm, then turn them out on to a cooling rack.

5 Allow the cakes to cool completely before filling. Whisk the cream until fairly stiff, then fold in the maple syrup. Spoon this on top of one of the cakes and spread it out evenly, leaving a border – this allows for the cream to be squashed down by the top layer of cake without spilling over too much. If your berries are all about the same size, simply dot them over the cream. If you are using strawberries of different sizes, cut them up first.

6 Place the other cake on top and decorate with more fruit if you like.

225g unsalted butter, softened
225g wholemeal spelt flour
2 heaped tsp baking powder
3 large eggs
225g maple syrup
seeds scraped from ½ split
   vanilla pod

Filling
150g double cream
1 tbsp maple syrup
250g strawberries, raspberries
   or other summer fruit

Almond and lemon fairy cakes

Everyone loves a fairy cake and these are another triumph for spelt flour. You can just spoon the decoration on top or make them into butterfly cakes like we did. Delicious either way. For a change, you could also make the cakes with orange juice instead of lemon.

1 Preheat the oven to 180°C/160°C Fan/Gas 4. Line a 12-hole fairy cake tray with paper cases.

2 Put the spelt flour, ground almonds and baking powder in a bowl and whisk to combine them thoroughly and remove any lumps.

3 Beat the butter with an electric whisk in a separate bowl or in a stand mixer for 4–5 minutes until it's very fluffy and white. Add a spoonful of the flour and almonds to the butter, then an egg, whisking well in between each addition. Add the remaining egg, then more flour and almonds, again whisking well.

4 Fold in the remaining flour and almonds, then add the maple syrup, lemon zest and juice and the almond extract, if using. The mixture should have a fairly wet consistency so it drops off the spoon.

5 Divide the mixture between the cases, then bake the cakes in the oven for 15–20 minutes until well risen and golden brown. Remove them from the oven, then take the cakes out of the tray and place them on a cooling rack.

6 Mix the mascarpone with the maple syrup. When the cakes are cool, dollop a spoonful of the mixture on top of each one, then add a little lemon curd.

7 If you'd like to make butterfly cakes, cut a small round from the top of each cake and slice it in half to make wings. Fill the hollow with the cream and curd, then place the wings on top.

Makes 12

50g wholemeal spelt flour
50g ground almonds
1 tsp baking powder
100g unsalted butter, softened
2 eggs
100g maple syrup
zest of 1 lemon
1 tbsp lemon juice
a few drops of almond extract (optional)

Decoration
150g mascarpone cheese
1 tbsp maple syrup
Davina's lemon curd (see page 215)

Brownies

Brownies without refined sugar? Could this be true? These are amazing I promise you and I am a big brownie fan. The texture is slightly different from usual but still delicious. Add chopped nuts if you like or a shot of espresso coffee along with the milk. The darker the chocolate the better, and you can now buy the 100% stuff in supermarkets.

1 Preheat the oven to 190°C/170°C Fan/Gas 5. Grease a 30cm x 20cm brownie tin and line it with baking parchment. Leave the paper sticking up at the sides to make it easier to lift the brownie out when it's cooked.

2 Put the chocolate, milk, butter, honey, maple syrup and vanilla seeds in a saucepan. Warm over a very gentle heat, stirring regularly, until everything has melted and you have a rich, glossy-looking batter. Remove the pan from the heat and whisk in the cocoa powder.

3 Allow the mixture to cool for a couple of minutes, then beat in the eggs. Finally, add the flour and baking powder. The mixture at this point will look grainier than usual because of the texture of the flour.

4 Pour the mixture into the prepared tin and bake it in the oven for about 15 minutes until it is just set in the middle but still nice and gooey. Remove the tin from the oven and use the baking paper to help you slide the whole brownie on to a cooling rack as soon as possible so it doesn't continue to cook. Cut into squares when cool.

Davina's tip
For a real treat, try swirling some home-made dulce de leche (see page 214) into the mixture with a skewer. Mouthwateringly good.

Makes about 15 squares

125g dark chocolate (100% cocoa)
100ml milk
100g unsalted butter, plus extra
　for greasing the tin
175g honey
150g maple syrup
seeds scraped from ½ split
　vanilla pod
50g cocoa powder, sieved
3 eggs
150g wholemeal spelt flour
1 tsp baking powder

Digestive biscuits

Crazy delicious, guilt-free biscuits, these are perfect for dunking. Digestives are my very favourites and these taste like a biscuit should.

1 Put the flour, oats, baking powder and a pinch of salt in a food processor and blitz them – you want a mixture that's just slightly coarser than flour. Add the butter and pulse until the mixture resembles fine breadcrumbs, then tip it all into a bowl.

2 Add the maple syrup and gently work it into the mixture until you have a dough. Don't worry if it's very soft, as it will firm up in the fridge. Wrap the dough in cling film and chill it in the fridge for at least an hour.

3 Preheat the oven to 190°C/170°C Fan/Gas 5. Line 2 baking trays with baking parchment. Generously flour your work surface.

4 Divide the dough in half, then rewrap one piece and put it back in the fridge. Roll out the remaining half and, using a cutter about the size of a digestive biscuit, cut out circles. Re-roll the offcuts, making sure you use plenty of flour to prevent sticking. You should end up with 12 biscuits.

5 Remove the rest of the dough from the fridge and repeat to make another 12 biscuits. Place the biscuits on the baking trays.

6 Bake the biscuits for 15–20 minutes until they're golden brown and crisp. Keep a very close eye on them, as a minute too long could mean they overcook. Remove the biscuits from the oven and immediately transfer them to a wire rack to cool.

Makes about 24

200g wholemeal flour, plus extra for dusting the work surface
200g oats
1 tsp baking powder
pinch of salt
200g unsalted butter, well chilled and cut into cubes
150g maple syrup

Flapjacks

These are a party in the mouth. Make them and I'm sure you'll agree.

1 Preheat the oven to 180°C/160°C Fan/Gas 4. Line a 30 x 20cm tin with baking parchment.

2 Put the butter, honey and dates in a saucepan over a low heat. Melt them together, crushing the dates with a wooden spoon so they break up into the butter and honey and get all lovely and squidgy. Stir in the oats and coconut and mix thoroughly.

3 Pack the mixture into the prepared tin and bake for 20–25 minutes until golden brown. The flapjacks will still seem soft at this point, but don't worry – they'll firm up once cool.

4 Remove the tin from the oven and immediately score the surface into about 15 squares. Leave the flapjack to cool in the tin, then cut it into squares.

Makes about 15 squares

200g unsalted butter
250ml honey
150g chopped dates
400g porridge oats
100g desiccated coconut

Fruit tea bread

A lovely old-fashioned bake, this is a great thing to serve up at teatime when you fancy a little something. Spread with lashings of good butter. It's easy to make but you just need to remember to soak the fruit beforehand.

1 Put the dried fruit in a bowl and pour over the tea and maple syrup. Leave the fruit to soak in the tea and syrup for at least a few hours and preferably overnight.

2 Preheat the oven to 180°C/160°C Fan/Gas 4. Line a 1kg/2lb loaf tin with baking parchment.

3 Sieve the flour into a bowl and stir in the baking powder and mixed spice. Add the fruit and any unabsorbed liquid along with the eggs. Mix everything thoroughly, then spoon into the prepared loaf tin.

4 Bake the tea bread in the oven for about an hour. Remove and leave it to cool in the tin for 10 minutes, then turn it out and transfer it to a cooling rack.

5 Serve thickly sliced and spread with butter.

350g dried fruit (mixture of raisins, chopped dried apricots, sultanas, dates)
200ml freshly brewed tea
50ml maple syrup
250g wholemeal spelt flour
2 tsp baking powder
1 tsp mixed spice
2 eggs

Banoffee pie

When we started working on this book I put it out there that I wanted to include a banoffee pie – which is my favourite pudding in the whole wide world – made without white table sugar. I didn't believe it could be done, but it has and it's amazing. The thing is that the usual banoffee pie is so sweet you can't eat much of it. Good news – you can eat more of this one! Remember to leave the dulce de leche out of the fridge for a while before using or it will be hard to spread. And try not to eat it while it's waiting.

1 For the base, blitz the biscuits and the pecans together in a food processor or blender. Melt the butter in a saucepan, then add the biscuits and pecans and mix thoroughly. Tip the mixture into a 23cm loose-bottomed flan tin and press it down well, then put it in the fridge to chill and set – this will take at least half an hour.

2 To assemble, spread the base with dulce de leche, then put the pie back in the fridge to set for half an hour.

3 When it's set, take the pie out of the fridge and arrange the bananas on top. Whisk the cream until it forms soft peaks, then pile it on top of the bananas. Drizzle over some chocolate sauce (use the fondue mix on page 186) if you feel extra greedy.

Serves 6

Base
150g Davina's digestive biscuits (see page 177)
50g pecan nuts
50g butter

Topping
1 portion of Davina's dulce de leche (see page 214), at room temperature
4 small bananas, sliced
300ml double or whipping cream
chocolate sauce (optional)

Chocolate mousse

A corker of a recipe to crack out at a dinner party, this mousse is so good
that no one can quite believe it doesn't contain refined sugar. Do get hold
of some 100% dark choc to make it – anything under 100% contains sugar.
The honey will affect the flavour so vary it as you like – chestnut, lavender
or thyme are all nice.

1 Break the chocolate into small pieces with a sharp knife and put
them in a saucepan with the honey, cream and vanilla seeds.

2 Warm gently over a very low heat until the chocolate has completely
melted and has combined well with the other ingredients. Remove
from the heat and beat in the egg yolks.

3 Whisk the egg whites until they have reached the stiff peak stage.
Using a metal spoon, put a quarter of the whites into the chocolate
mixture and stir them in lightly to loosen everything up a bit. Stir in
the rest of the egg whites, again treating the mixture as lightly as
possible so you don't knock the air out of it.

4 Divide the mixture between 8 small ramekins and chill for several
hours before eating.

- -

Davina's tip
Try adding some instant espresso powder dissolved in a tablespoon
of hot water or add a few drops of orange, rose or peppermint oil.
Peppermint is particularly good and makes the mousse seem sweeter.

Serves 8

60g chocolate (100% cocoa)
40g strong-flavoured honey
150ml double cream
seeds scraped from ½ split
   vanilla pod
2 eggs, separated

Chocolate fondue

A no-brainer. This is really a multi-purpose chocolate sauce that's great used for fondue but can also be drizzled over things such as banoffee pie (see page 182). And if you put it in a jar in the fridge it will set softly, so you can use it as a chocolate spread. The fried cake for dipping works best if the cake is frozen first, as you will then get cleaner, less crumbly pieces to work with.

1 To make the fondue sauce, put all the ingredients in a saucepan and melt them together, stirring regularly until very smooth.

2 Transfer the sauce to a fondue pot or a serving bowl and put it on the table if using for fondue. Otherwise pour the mixture into a sterilised glass jar and keep it in the fridge. Reheat to use as a sauce.

3 To make the fried cake, cut the cakes into cubes – each fairy cake could be cut into 4 pieces.

4 Melt the butter in a frying pan. Whisk the egg thoroughly with the maple syrup in a bowl. Soak the pieces of cake in the egg and maple syrup mixture, then remove them and fry them in the butter, turning them so they brown on all sides. Drain on kitchen towel and serve the fried cake with the chocolate fondue and the fruit.

Fondue sauce
100g chocolate (100% cocoa)
100g maple syrup
25g butter
150ml double cream
75ml milk

To serve
fairy cakes made with orange
    juice (see page 173), frozen
15g butter
1 egg
1 tbsp maple syrup
fruit, such as strawberries,
    cherries, chunks of mango,
    pineapple, peach, banana

Lime and ginger cheesecake

My husband loves key lime pie and cheesecake and this recipe brings the two together – and a smile to his face! You do need some of my digestive biscuits (see page 177), but the cheesecake itself is easy to make and doesn't need any cooking.

1 Blitz the digestive biscuits in a food processor or put them in a plastic bag and bash them with a rolling pin until they are the consistency of fine breadcrumbs.

2 Melt the butter in a saucepan. Remove the pan from the heat and add the ground ginger and crushed biscuits, then stir until the mixture is well combined. Press the mixture into a 23cm flan dish and put it in the fridge to chill while you make the filling.

3 Break up the cream cheese with a fork to loosen it a little. Put the double cream in a large bowl and whisk until slightly thickened but not really stiff. Add the cream cheese, zest and juice of the limes and the maple syrup and mix well. Pour this over the biscuit base and spread it out as evenly as possible.

4 Chill the cheesecake for a few hours or preferably overnight until firm. This is also good frozen – just put it in the freezer and remove it about half an hour before serving.

Serves 8

200g home-made digestive
    biscuits (see page 177)
75g butter
1 tsp ground ginger

Filling
300g cream cheese
250ml double cream
grated zest and juice of 2 limes
100ml maple syrup

Peach and almond crumble

We're talking peach here but you could use any seasonal fruit, such as apples or plums. I've also tried using crumbled digestives (see my recipe on page 177) instead of the almonds and that worked a treat.

1 Preheat the oven to 180°C/160°C Fan/Gas 4.

2 Slice the peaches. Grease a 1-litre baking dish with butter and arrange the peaches in the bottom of it. If you think your peaches need a little extra sweetness, drizzle them with maple syrup.

3 For the topping, put the flour in a bowl, add the diced butter and rub it into the flour with your fingertips until the mixture is the consistency of breadcrumbs. Stir in the ground and flaked almonds, then drizzle over the maple syrup and stir briefly. You'll think the mixture seems a little strange without sugar, but don't worry – it will be fine.

4 Spoon the crumble mixture on top of the peaches, then bake in the oven for about 30 minutes, until the top is tinged with brown. Serve with home-made custard (see page 215).

Serves 4–6

3 ripe peaches, skinned and stoned
butter, for greasing
a drizzle of maple syrup (optional)

Crumble topping
175g wholemeal spelt flour
65g cold butter, diced
25g ground almonds
25g flaked almonds
50ml maple syrup

Blackberry and apple pie

This is a proper double-crust pie and the buttery spelt pastry works beautifully. It's the perfect autumn pud to make if you've gathered some blackberries but you can make it with just apple if you like. Great with home-made custard (see page 215), of course.

1 First make the pastry. Sift the flour into a bowl and add a pinch of salt. Add the butter and rub it in with your fingertips until the mixture has the consistency of fine breadcrumbs. Add the egg yolk, mix briefly, then add the water a teaspoon at a time, mixing it in until you have a soft, pliable dough.

2 Divide the pastry in 2, making 1 piece slightly bigger than the other. Wrap the pieces in cling film and leave them to chill in the fridge for half an hour.

3 Preheat the oven to 180°C/160°C Fan/Gas 4. Put a baking sheet into the oven to heat at the same time.

4 Roll out the larger piece of pastry on a floured work surface and use it to line the base of your pie dish. Make sure you roll it big enough to overlap the edges of the dish – you can trim it later.

5 Peel, core and thinly slice the apples. Put them in a bowl and add the lemon juice to stop the apples turning brown. Add the blackberries to the bowl. Whisk a pinch of cinnamon into the maple syrup, then pour this over the fruit. Turn everything over so the fruit is completely covered in the syrup, then pile it all into the pastry-lined pie dish.

6 Roll out the other piece of pastry. Wet the edges of the bottom layer of pastry with water and place the top layer over the pie. Trim the edges of the pastry, then press them together, either with a fork or your fingers. Brush the top with milk to glaze.

7 Place the pie on the preheated baking tray and bake it in the oven for 30–35 minutes until the pastry is lovely and golden brown and the fruit has softened. This is so good.

Serves 6

700g Bramley apples
   (2–3 medium apples)
juice of ½ lemon
300g blackberries
pinch of cinnamon
up to 75ml maple syrup
1 tbsp milk, to glaze

Pastry

250g wholemeal spelt flour,
   plus extra for dusting the
   work surface
pinch of salt
150g cold butter, cubed
1 egg yolk
1–2 tbsp ice-cold water or milk

Baked apples

You can use other apples but Bramleys are by far and away the best, as they go all fluffy and lovely as they bake. This is quick and easy to make and always good to eat.

1 Preheat the oven to 180°C/160°C Fan/Gas 4. Grease a large ovenproof dish with butter.

2 Core the apples, leaving them intact at the base so the filling doesn't come out. Do this by cutting down around the core from the top but leaving the last centimetre in place. Stand the apples upright in the dish.

3 Stuff the apples with the raisins. Heat the honey or maple syrup with the cinnamon and pour this into the centre of each apple over the raisins. Dot a small piece of butter on top of each apple.

4 Bake the apples in the oven for 35–40 minutes. Serve them in bowls and spoon over any juices from the dish. Lovely with custard (see page 215) or crème fraiche.

Serves 4

a few knobs of butter, plus extra
  for greasing
4 large Bramley apples
50g raisins
2 tbsp honey or maple syrup
pinch of cinnamon

Honey and vanilla panna cotta

I know this might not be light on calories but I wanted to make a panna cotta without table sugar and this works! I used to avoid any recipe that mentioned gelatine for some reason, but once I plucked up the courage to try it I found it was no trouble at all. Vanilla pods were another thing that worried me and I always used to use vanilla extract instead, but I've discovered that the extract contains sugar. So I've conquered my fear of the pods, which give a fantastic sweetness to a dish. Sometimes you add a whole pod for flavour but it's usually just the seeds. Simply run a spoon or your thumb down the middle of the split pod and scrape the little black seeds into your mixture.

1 Prepare 4 ramekins or moulds by brushing the insides with a little vegetable oil and then lightly wiping them over with kitchen towel.

2 Soak the gelatine in a small bowl of cold water.

3 Put the cream, milk, buttermilk and honey in a saucepan. Scrape in the seeds from the vanilla pod, then heat gently, stirring until the honey has melted. Leave to cool a little, then take the gelatine from the bowl, squeeze out the water and add the gelatine to the cream mixture. Stir over a gentle heat until the gelatine is completely dissolved but do not let the mixture boil.

4 Strain the mixture through a sieve into a jug, then divide it between the ramekins. Leave them to cool, then chill for at least 4 hours by which time they should be set.

5 To serve, dip the ramekins into some very hot water for a few seconds, then turn the panna cottas out on to plates. If you like, drizzle them with some extra honey before serving.

Makes 4

vegetable oil, for brushing
2 sheets of leaf gelatine
300ml double cream
100ml whole milk
50ml buttermilk
75g honey, plus extra for serving
seeds from ½ split vanilla pod

Citrus bread and butter pudding

A touch of citrus brings a bread and butter pudding to life. People always say that this is a great way of using up stale bread, but who needs an excuse? It's just good.

1 Preheat the oven to 180°C/160°C Fan/Gas 4. Butter a 1-litre ovenproof dish.

2 Put the raisins in a small saucepan and cover them with the orange juice. Bring the juice to the boil, then remove the pan from the heat and leave the raisins to soak until cool.

3 Mix the milk, cream, eggs and maple syrup in a bowl and add the orange zest. Strain the raisins and set them aside, then add the orange juice to the egg mixture.

4 Butter the bread and arrange a layer of it in the dish, butter-side down. Sprinkle over the raisins, then arrange the rest of the bread on top, this time butter-side up. Pour over the egg and cream mixture, making sure it soaks through to the bottom layer.

5 Drizzle a little more maple syrup over the bread, then grate in some nutmeg. Bake the pudding in the oven for 30–40 minutes until the custard has set and the top layer of bread is well browned and crisp.

Davina's tip
To make this pudding even more zingy you could spread the bread with my home-made lemon curd (see page 215).

Serves 6

butter, for greasing and spreading
50g raisins
juice and grated zest of 1 orange
200ml whole milk
100ml double cream
3 eggs
25g maple syrup, plus more
   for drizzling
8 thin slices of wholemeal bread,
   crusts removed, cut into triangles
nutmeg

Compotes

I love having fresh fruit compotes in the fridge. They're great with yoghurt or porridge for breakfast and also make a perfect pud with custard or crème fraiche later in the day. Try stirring some compote through whipped cream for an instant fruit fool. You'll thank me, I promise.

Blueberry and lime compote

1 Put the blueberries in a saucepan with the lime zest and juice and 100ml of water. Add a tablespoon of honey and slowly bring to the boil.

2 Reduce the temperature and simmer for a few minutes until the liquid has turned a deep purple colour and some of the blueberries have burst. Taste and add a little more honey if you think the compote needs it.

3 This compote can also be thickened to use as a topping for cheesecakes, pancakes or flans. To thicken, mix the arrowroot with a little cold water. Add this mixture to the blueberries and heat gently, stirring constantly, until the sauce has thickened and is very glossy.

400g blueberries
zest and juice of 1 lime
2 tbsp honey (to taste)

To thicken (if required)
2 tsp arrowroot

Plum compote

1 Put the plums, spices and maple syrup in a saucepan with 50ml of water and bring to the boil. Turn down the heat and cover the pan with a lid. Simmer for about 15 minutes until the plums have softened but haven't completely collapsed.

2 You can eat the compote as it is, but you'll find that once the plums are cooked the skins will either have fallen off or slip off very easily, so you can remove them before serving if you prefer. You can also reduce the liquid by simmering the compote uncovered for 10–15 minutes. This gives you something that's halfway between compote and jam.

800g firm but ripe plums, halved
   and stoned
1 star anise
1 cinnamon stick
2 cloves
125ml maple syrup

Clafoutis

I wasn't sure about including a clafoutis recipe but my girlfriends were all shocked, saying 'What kind of French person are you? You have to have a clafoutis.' So I did, and they were right. It's very good.

1 Preheat the oven to 180°C/160°C Fan/Gas 4. Grease a 23cm round, shallow ovenproof dish with butter. Don't use a loose-bottomed tin as the batter will run out!

2 Spread the cherries evenly over the base of the dish.

3 Put the spelt flour and almonds in a bowl and add a pinch of salt. Whisk in the eggs, followed by the milk, double cream, maple syrup and almond extract, if using. Pour this batter over the cherries.

4 Bake the clafoutis in the oven for 25–30 minutes, until it's golden brown and slightly puffed up. Best served warm with double cream.

Serves 6

butter, for greasing
500g cherries, pitted
50g wholemeal spelt flour
50g ground almonds
pinch of salt
2 eggs, beaten
200ml whole milk
100ml double cream
75ml maple syrup
½ tsp almond extract (optional)

Maple and pecan tarts

These are a sort of cross between trad English treacle tart and American pecan pie – something dear to my husband's heart. A bit naughty but there's no table sugar, just maple syrup. You have to bake the pastry cases before adding the filling so you'll need baking beans to hold the pastry down so it doesn't puff up. You can buy ceramic ones but ordinary dried beans work just as well. You also need four 12cm tartlet tins.

1 To make the pastry, put the flour and salt in a bowl or a food processor. Add the butter and either rub it in with your fingertips or blitz it until the mixture is the consistency of fine breadcrumbs. Add the egg yolk and 1 tablespoon of the water and mix together. If the dough is too crumbly, add a little more water. Wrap the dough in cling film and chill for at least an hour. If you are in a hurry, chill the dough in the freezer for 10–15 minutes.

2 Preheat the oven to 200°C/180°C Fan/Gas 6. Divide the pastry into 4 balls. Dust your work surface with flour and roll the balls out into rounds to fit your tins. Line the tartlet tins with the pastry, then pierce the bases all over with a fork. Cover each pastry case with a circle of baking parchment, scatter in some baking beans, then chill for 10 minutes in the freezer.

3 Put the tins on a baking tray and bake in the preheated oven for 15 minutes. Remove the beans and paper, then bake for another 10 minutes until the pastry is cooked through and light brown in colour. When cool, trim the edges of the pastry if necessary.

4 To make the filling, melt the maple syrup and butter together in a saucepan. Add the orange juice and zest, then stir in the breadcrumbs and pecans. Divide the filling between the pastry cases, then bake the tarts in the oven for 15–20 minutes, until golden brown. The tops will be puffed up and feel very soft when you remove the tarts from the oven, but don't worry, they will firm up as they cool.

5 Serve warm with custard (see page 215) or cold with crème fraiche.

Davina's tip
These look pretty scattered with some extra orange zest before serving.

Serves 4

Filling
200ml maple syrup
50g butter
juice and grated zest of ½ orange
50g wholemeal breadcrumbs
50g pecan nuts, finely chopped

Pastry
200g wholemeal spelt flour, plus
    extra for dusting the work surface
pinch of salt
110g cold butter, cubed
1 egg yolk
1–2 tbsp cold water

Glazed oranges with almonds

A fresh, pretty dessert, this is perfect to serve after a big meal.

1 First, slice off the top and bottom of an orange to make a flat surface. Then following the curve of the fruit, cut off the skin from top to bottom. Slice the orange into rounds, removing any pips or large pieces of pith as you go. Repeat with the rest of the oranges. You can divide some into segments if you prefer.

2 Put the orange slices on a serving plate or divide them between 4 bowls. Put the almonds in a dry frying pan and toast them lightly, shaking the pan so they don't burn. Set the almonds aside.

3 Put the butter and honey in a saucepan and heat them gently. When both have melted, turn up the heat and boil them for a couple of minutes. Remove the pan from the heat and whisk thoroughly until the butter and honey are completely combined. Add a few drops of rosewater, if using.

4 Pour the sauce over the oranges, then sprinkle the almonds on top. Add a few sprigs of mint and some rose petals, if you have them, and serve with some crème fraiche on the side.

Serves 4

6 oranges
75g flaked almonds
75g butter
75g honey
a few drops of rosewater (optional)

To serve
a few sprigs of mint
a few dried rose petals (optional)
crème fraiche

Davina's favourites

8 Basics

"If I can make my own chicken stock and my own sugar-free ketchup and mayo, so can you. You won't believe how easy it is."

Chicken stock

I was probably in my mid-30s before I dared to make a stock, but now I never let a chicken carcass go to waste. Home-made stock tastes SO good.

1 Put the chicken carcass and wings, if using, in a large saucepan. Cover with at least 1.5 litres of water and bring it to the boil. Skim off any starchy brown foam that collects on the surface of the liquid and keep skimming until the foam is white.

2 Add the vegetables, peppercorns and bay leaves. Turn the heat down very low and simmer for about 2 hours until you have a light brown stock. Strain the liquid through a fine sieve into a container.

3 The stock can be used immediately, but if you want to remove any fat, leave the stock in the fridge overnight. The fat will harden and collect at the top and is easily skimmed off. This stock freezes well.

1 chicken carcass (left from roasting a chicken)
4 chicken wings (optional)
2 carrots, broken in half
1 onion, quartered
2 celery sticks, broken in half
a few peppercorns
2 bay leaves

Home-made mayonnaise

There's sugar in all the prepared stuff and mayo just doesn't need it, so it's great to make your own. This does keep for a week or more, but if you want a smaller amount, use 1 egg yolk and 150ml of oil.

1 Fold up a tea towel and put it on your work surface, then place a mixing bowl on top. The tea towel will help the bowl stay in place while you're whisking.

2 Put the egg yolks in the mixing bowl and season them with salt. Add the mustard and mix together briefly with a whisk.

3 Start adding the oil, a few drops at a time, whisking constantly until the egg yolks have completely absorbed the oil before adding more. When you have used about a third of the oil, you can start adding a little more at a time until it's a steady stream. When all the oil is incorporated, add a squeeze of lemon juice.

4 You can make mayonnaise in a food processor in exactly the same way, adding a few drops of oil at a time, then gradually adding more.

5 Store the mayonnaise in the fridge in a bowl covered with cling film.

2 egg yolks
pinch of salt
½ tsp Dijon mustard
300ml oil – groundnut, sunflower or corn (olive is too strong)
squeeze of lemon juice

- -

Davina's tip
If you find the mayonnaise is getting too stiff to work with, add a few drops of warm water at intervals.

Béchamel sauce

This is my basic béchamel sauce, which can be used in all sorts of dishes. It's made with spelt flour, which gives it a slightly flecky, brown look but that's no problem. There are loads of variations you can do, including adding herbs (see fish pie on page 103), cheese (see cauliflower cheese on page 140) or cream and poaching liquid (see chicken pot pie on page 108).

1 Melt the butter in a saucepan over a gentle heat. Add the flour and stir it thoroughly into the butter. Stir for a couple of minutes to cook the flour – this is important, as the flour can taste raw if not toasted in this way first.

2 Gradually add the milk about 100ml at a time, stirring constantly in between each addition, until it is all incorporated and you have a smooth if runny sauce.

3 Turn up the heat slightly and continue to stir the sauce until it comes to the boil and thickens. Season with salt and pepper and remove the pan from the heat.

50g butter
50g wholemeal spelt flour
500ml whole milk
salt and black pepper

- -

Davina's tip
If you need to store the béchamel for any length of time before using, put a layer of cling film over it, making sure it comes into contact with the surface area of the sauce. This will prevent a skin from forming. If a skin does form, just give the sauce a vigorous whisk and the skin will disperse into the sauce.

Home-made tomato ketchup

I never dreamed I could make my own ketchup but I have. It's different from the classic but it's good, free of added table sugar and keeps well in the fridge for a couple of weeks. A bouquet garni is the French name for a bundle of herbs and spices you add to the other ingredients for flavour.

1 First make the bouquet garni. Put all the ingredients in a small square of fine cloth, such as muslin, and tie it into a little bag with some string.

2 Put the tomatoes in a saucepan with the cider vinegar, onion and garlic. Bash the bouquet garni with a rolling pin or the back of a knife briefly to start releasing the aromatic oils from the spices, then add it to the pan. Add the cinnamon and smoked paprika, then season with salt and pepper.

3 Simmer the tomatoes, uncovered, until they're well reduced – for about 45 minutes – stirring regularly to make sure they don't catch on the bottom. Remove the pan from the heat and fish out the bouquet garni. Allow the tomatoes to cool a little, then purée them until very smooth and tip the mixture back into the pan. If you don't think your blender or food processor has done a good enough job, push the pulp through a sieve.

4 Add the maple syrup and 50ml of water to the tomatoes. Simmer for 5 minutes, stirring regularly, then taste. Add a little more maple syrup if you think the mixture needs it, and adjust the seasoning if necessary. Keep simmering and stirring the ketchup until it almost seems dry and you think it is in danger of catching on the bottom, despite the stirring.

5 Spoon the ketchup into a sterilised jar and when it has cooled down, put it in the fridge. If it separates slightly, simply stir the liquid back into the sauce.

Davina's tip
Before putting home-made ketchup, jam or any other preserves in jars the jars must be clean and sterilised. Wash them well in hot soapy water. Heat the oven to 140°C/120°C Fan/Gas 1. Put the jars on a baking tray and put them in the oven for about 10 minutes. Remove them carefully – they'll be hot! If you're using the lids of the jars, boil them in a pan of water for 10 minutes.

2 x 400g cans of chopped tomatoes
1 tbsp cider vinegar
1 large onion, finely chopped
2 garlic cloves, finely chopped
bouquet garni (see below)
small pinch of cinnamon
pinch of sweet smoked paprika
1 tbsp maple syrup
  (more if you like)
salt and black pepper

Bouquet garni
2 cloves
1 tsp allspice berries
1 blade of mace
1 tsp celery seeds
1 tsp black peppercorns
2 bay leaves

Teriyaki sauce

Some bottles of soy sauce contain added sugar so check before you buy. Most of the good ones don't.

1 Put all the ingredients in a small saucepan. Bring them to the boil, then turn the heat down and simmer for about 10 minutes, until the liquid has reduced by half and is syrupy. I like this sauce not too sweet, but have a taste and add more honey if you like.

2 Strain the sauce to remove the ginger and garlic, then pour it into a sterilised jar (see page 212). It will keep indefinitely in the fridge.

200ml light soy sauce or tamari
200ml mirin or pineapple juice
1 tsp rice wine or cider vinegar
1 tbsp honey (more if you like)
15g fresh root ginger, peeled and sliced
3 fat garlic cloves, sliced

Moroccan spice mix

1 Put the whole spices in a dry frying pan and fry them for a couple of minutes, shaking the pan regularly, until you smell their aroma. Immediately remove the pan from the heat and tip the spices on to a plate to cool.

2 Grind the toasted spices in a spice or coffee grinder or with a pestle and mortar, then mix in the ground spices. Tip the mixture into a sterilised jar (see page 212) and store it in a cool, dark place.

2 tbsp cumin seeds
1 tbsp coriander seeds
4 cloves
2 tsp ground ginger
1 tsp ground cinnamon
½ tsp turmeric
½ tsp cayenne (optional)

Davina's spice blend

1 Put all the whole spices in a dry frying pan. Fry them for a couple of minutes, shaking the pan regularly, until you start to smell the aromas. Immediately remove the pan from the heat and tip the spices on to a plate to cool.

2 Grind the spices in a spice or coffee grinder or with a pestle and mortar, then stir in the turmeric and cinnamon. Tip the mixture into a sterilised jar (see page 212) and store it somewhere fairly cool and dark.

1 tbsp fennel seeds
1 tbsp coriander seeds
1 tbsp cumin seeds
1 tbsp fenugreek
1 tsp white peppercorns
1 blade of mace or ¼ tsp nutmeg
1 bay leaf
4 cardamom pods
4 cloves
1 tsp turmeric
½ tsp cinnamon

Fruit coulis

Any soft fruit can be used for coulis but raspberries and strawberries probably work best. Once made, the coulis can be kept in the fridge for up to a week but it also freezes well.

1 Rinse the fruit well and if using strawberries, hull them and cut them in half.

2 Put the berries in a saucepan with the honey and lemon juice. Heat very gently until the fruit releases most of its juices into the melting honey and lemon. This will only take a couple of minutes for raspberries and up to 10 minutes for strawberries.

3 Remove the pan from the heat and purée the fruit. Push the purée through a sieve back into the saucepan and taste. Add a little more honey if necessary and let it melt very gently to combine. Let the coulis cool, then eat, store or freeze as you like.

500g raspberries or strawberries
1 tsp honey
juice of 1 lemon

- -

Davina's tip
I like to freeze fruit coulis in ice cube trays. Once the cubes are frozen, I tip them into freezer bags so I can defrost a few when I need them.

Dulce de leche

I have to confess I do have a sweet tooth and this is one of my favourite naughty but nice treats. There's no table sugar in this recipe so it's not quite as sweet as usual, but it's good and easy to make – it just needs a lot of stirring and I mean a lot. You can use coconut milk instead of evaporated if you want a change of flavour.

1 Pour the evaporated milk and syrup into a saucepan. Bring them to the boil, then turn the heat down and simmer, stirring regularly, until the sauce has reduced and thickened to the consistency of a thick pouring custard. This will take 20 minutes to half an hour so be patient.

2 Remove the pan from the heat and pour the sauce into a sterilised jar (see page 212). Leave it to cool and it will set to a spreadable consistency. This keeps well in the fridge for at least a few weeks.

410g can of evaporated milk
150ml maple syrup

Lemon curd

Who doesn't love lemon curd? But the bought stuff contains loads of sugar so I make my own. You can also use oranges, limes or passion fruit.

1 Melt the honey or maple syrup in a saucepan with the butter. Remove the pan from the heat and leave the mixture to cool for a few minutes, then add the remaining ingredients.

2 Put the pan back on the heat and stir until the mixture has thickened. It will seem quite runny for a few minutes, but then will suddenly thicken up to the consistency of custard. Stir or whisk constantly to prevent the eggs from curdling.

3 Put the curd through a sieve to remove the zest and any small lumps of egg. Pour it into a sterilised jar (see page 212) and allow to cool, then refrigerate until needed. The curd should keep for a few weeks.

150g honey or maple syrup
100g butter
zest of 1 well-scrubbed lemon
juice of 4 lemons (about 100ml)
4 eggs, lightly beaten

Custard

My family likes custard with crumbles and other puds and this home-made version is so much better than the powdered stuff. Try it and see.

1 Put the milk and the vanilla seeds into a saucepan. Heat gently until the milk is getting close to boiling (you'll see tiny bubbles start to appear), then remove the pan from the heat.

2 Put the egg yolks in a bowl, add a tablespoon of maple syrup and whisk until well combined.

3 If a skin has formed on the milk, peel it off. Add a small ladleful of milk to the eggs and stir to combine, then add the rest of the milk and pour the whole lot back into the saucepan.

4 Put the pan over a low to medium heat and stir constantly for several minutes until the custard has thickened – keep a close eye on it, as it will happen suddenly. To check whether the custard is the right consistency, coat the back of your wooden spoon. If, when you draw your finger along the back of the spoon, the line remains, the custard is thick enough.

5 Taste the custard and add more maple syrup if you need to. The custard should not be very sweet. Strain the custard into a jug.

350ml whole milk
seeds scraped from ½ split
   vanilla pod
4 egg yolks
1–2 tbsp maple syrup

5 Weeks to Sugar-Free

Like everyone, I'm super-busy and I know that cooking meals for the family from scratch can seem daunting. I find that if I get organised and plan ahead it makes life easier and avoids waste! I hate waste. So to help us all, I've made a 5 week menu plan, using the recipes in this book. It's designed to help you gradually reduce the amount of sugar in your diet.

The aim is to cut out the sugar we add to food, or is added by manufacturers, because those are the most damaging in terms of our health, plus the sugar naturally present in honey, syrups and fruit juices. There's also natural sugar in whole fruit, starchy vegetables and dairy products but it comes packaged with other important nutrients like vitamins and minerals so it's not necessary or sensible to cut out these foods as well. The good news is that as you progress though the 5 weeks your taste buds will adapt and become more sensitive to sugar and you'll start to enjoy the natural flavours of food. Best to stop drinking alcohol for these 5 weeks too.

This is not a calorie-counted plan, but if you want to check the calorie content of recipes, have a look at the list on pages 219–220 and make changes to suit your needs. I've sometimes suggested having the same thing, such as a soup, two days running to save work, but that's up to you. Again, you can switch recipes around as you prefer.

Having some food in the freezer makes it less likely you'll get caught out and resort to the packaged stuff. Make double quantities of recipes such as ragù sauce and soups, then freeze them for those extra-busy days.

Week 1	Breakfast	Snack	Lunch	Snack	Evening meal
Monday	Home-made granola with whole milk	Fruit leather	French onion soup with toasted bread and cheese	Flapjack	Shepherd's pie + Pea purée
Tuesday	Poached eggs with avocado on toast	Banana	Bean salad; Melon	Digestive biscuit	Barley risotto with mushrooms and butternut squash
Wednesday	Home-made granola with whole milk	Power ball	Feta, watermelon and avocado salad; Blueberry and lime compote	Coconut and lime lolly	Ragù with spaghetti + green salad
Thursday	Bircher muesli with whole milk	Apple	Warm quinoa salad with avocado and broad beans	Roast beetroot dip with oatcakes	Burgers + Potato salad + Red slaw; Glazed oranges with almonds
Friday	Proper porridge with raspberries	Power ball	Chicken and vegetable soup; Fresh pineapple	Olives + raw vegetable sticks	Sea bass with mushrooms and potatoes
Saturday	American-style fluffy pancakes		Pitted bagels with cream cheese and smoked salmon; 2 plums	Digestive biscuit	Chicken with chickpeas and kale; Blackberry and apple pie
Sunday	Mediterranean frittata		Pea, pesto and spelt salad; Pomegranate	Mango lassi ice lolly	Slow-roast Moroccan lamb + Cannellini bean purée + green veg; Chocolate fondue

Week 2	Breakfast	Snack	Lunch	Snack	Evening meal
Monday	Proper porridge and blueberries	Pear	Roast tomato soup with mozzarella balls + Multigrain bread; Fresh pineapple	Strawberry and blueberry ice lolly	Glazed chicken wings + Creamy vegetable gratin
Tuesday	Bircher muesli with whole milk	2 plums	Bruschetta with mushroom and taleggio; Kiwi fruit	Roast beetroot dip with oatcakes	Risotto with spring vegetables
Wednesday	Poached eggs with avocado on toast	Banana	Home-made baked beans on toast; Fresh fruit salad	Oatcakes with cheese	Fish patties + Green beans with bacon + Sweet potato fries
Thursday	Bircher muesli with whole milk	Digestive biscuit	Chicken noodle soup + Multigrain bread	Power ball	Pork bean and sweet potato chilli
Friday	Crêpes	Power ball	Chicken noodle soup + oatcakes	Hummus with raw vegetable sticks	Roast tomato pasta + green salad
Saturday	Hash browns with fried or poached eggs		Halloumi, watercress and pomegranate salad	Fairy cake	Fish pie + Green beans with bacon and garlic; Honey panna cotta
Sunday	Pitted bagel with avocado, tomato and bacon filling		Rainbow salad	Fairy cake	Pot-roast chicken + Carrot and swede purée + Smashed new potatoes; Lime and ginger cheesecake

Week 3	Breakfast	Snack	Lunch	Snack	Evening meal
Monday	Toasted multigrain bread with butter + boiled egg	Fruit leather	Chicken noodle soup; Plain yoghurt + fresh berries	Fruit leather	Beef burgers + Cauliflower cheese + green salad
Tuesday	Proper porridge and raspberries	Digestive biscuit	Home-made baked beans on toast; Fresh pineapple	Hummus with raw vegetable sticks	Chicken pot pie + Pea purée
Wednesday	Home-made granola with whole milk	Banana	Pitted bagel with avocado tomato and bacon filling; Fresh mango	Guacamole with oatcakes	Barley risotto
Thursday	Poached eggs on toast	Power ball	Feta, watermelon and avocado salad	Fruit tea bread	Salmon with lentils and spinach
Friday	Proper porridge and banana	Plain yoghurt	Lentil and spinach soup; Fresh fruit salad	Fruit tea bread	Fish and chips
Saturday	Pea, asparagus and broad bean frittata		Lentil and spinach soup	Olives	Prawn cocktail in avocado boats; Cassoulet
Sunday	Pitted bagels with egg mayo filling		Pitta pizza; Nectarine	Vegetable crisps	Davina's roast chicken + Potato, root vegetable and garlic mash + steamed broccoli; Banoffee pie

Week 4	Breakfast	Snack	Lunch	Snack	Evening meal
Monday	Home-made granola with whole milk	Banana	Roast vegetable and couscous salad	Mango lassi ice lolly	Roast tomato pasta
Tuesday	Multigrain toast with butter + boiled egg	Apple	Rainbow salad	Roast beetroot dip with oatcakes	Chicken and roast vegetable tray bake
Wednesday	Proper porridge and strawberries	Plain yoghurt	Pea, pesto and spelt salad	Fruit tea bread	Ham hock with vegetables
Thursday	Bircher muesli with whole milk	Plain yoghurt	Ham and split pea soup	Hummus with raw vegetable sticks	Beef stir-fry
Friday	Multigrain toast with butter and mashed avocado	Flapjack	Ham and split pea soup	Power ball	Ragù with spaghetti
Saturday	Bacon and mushroom omelette		Warm quinoa salad with avocado and broad beans	Apple	Fish pie + greens with bacon
Sunday	Hash browns with grilled tomatoes		Roast tomato soup + Multigrain bread	Vegetable crisps	Figs with prosciutto and goat's cheese; Davina's roast chicken + Greens with bacon and garlic + Roast potatoes

Week 5	Breakfast	Snack	Lunch	Snack	Evening meal
Monday	Poached eggs with avocado on toast	Apple	Chicken and vegetable soup + Multigrain bread	Oatcakes with cheese	Beef stir-fry + brown rice
Tuesday	Bircher muesli with whole milk	Orange	Pitta pizza + mixed salad	Vegetable crisps	Pork bean and sweet potato chilli
Wednesday	Proper porridge with blueberries	Oatcakes with peanut butter	Bacon, bean and barley soup + Multigrain bread	Olives	Salmon with lentils + savoy cabbage
Thursday	Multigrain toast with butter + boiled egg	Plain yoghurt	Roast vegetable and couscous salad	Beetroot dip and vegetable sticks	Risotto with spring vegetables
Friday	Bircher muesli with whole milk	Banana	Bruschetta with broad bean topping	Vegetable crisps	Yoghurt-marinated chicken + Herby brown rice
Saturday	Chorizo frittata		Halloumi, watercress and pomegranate salad	Hummus and vegetable sticks	Sea bass with mushrooms and potatoes + green beans
Sunday	Kedgeree		Salmon niçoise	Vegetable crisps	Asparagus mimosa; Slow-roast Moroccan lamb + Roast root vegetables

Calorie Counts

Some people swear by calorie counting but others find it a real stress. I used to be a slave to my calorie counter, but now I prefer to concentrate on eating good healthy food, with no rubbish and as little sugar as poss. That keeps me trim without bothering with the sums. This book is not about calorie counting, but if you do like to keep a check on your daily calorie intake, here are the counts in kilocalories (kcal) for the recipes. They're listed in alphabetical order.

Almond and lemon fairy cakes: 256 kcal per cake
American-style fluffy pancakes: 60 kcal per pancake
Asparagus mimosa: 100 kcal per serving

Bacon and mushroom omelette: 430 kcal per serving
Bacon and mushroom omelette (with cheese: 534 kcal per serving
Bacon, bean and barley soup: 273 kcal per serving (4 portions); 182 kcal per serving (6 portions)
Baked apples: 151 kcal per serving
Banoffee pie: 707 kcal per serving
Barley risotto with mushrooms and butternut squash: 521 kcal per serving
Bean salad. 162 kcal per serving
Beef stir-fry: 300 kcal per serving
Bircher muesli: 352 kcal per serving
Blackberry and apple pie: 411 kcal per serving
Blueberry and lime compote: 95 kcal per serving (4 portions)
Brownies: 372 kcal per brownie
Brown shrimp and spinach tartlets: 636 kcal per serving
Bruschetta with broad bean and ricotta topping: 220 kcal per serving
Bruschetta with mushroom and taleggio topping: 236 kcal per serving
Burgers: 234 kcal per burger; 70 kcal per meatball; 175 kcal per slider

Cannellini bean purée: 182 kcal per serving
Carrot and swede purée: 72 kcal per serving
Cassoulet: 523 kcal per serving
Cauliflower cheese: 400 kcal per serving
Chicken and roast vegetable tray bake: 350 kcal per serving
Chicken and vegetable soup: 315 kcal per serving (4 portions); 210 kcal per serving (6 portions)
Chicken noodle soup: 243 kcal per serving (4 portions); 162 kcal per serving (6 portions)

Chicken pot pie: 585 kcal per serving
Chicken with chorizo, chickpeas and kale: 585 kcal per serving
Chocolate fondue: 1,752 kcal in total
Chocolate mousse: 164 kcal per serving
Chorizo frittata: 266 kcal per serving
Citrus bread and butter pudding: 290 kcal per serving
Clafoutis: 288 kcal per serving
Coconut and lime ice lollies: 148 kcal per lolly
Creamy vegetable gratin: 643 kcal per serving
Crêpes: 65 kcal per crêpe

Davina's roast chicken: 572 kcal per serving
Digestive biscuits. 138 kcal per biscuit

Feta, watermelon and avocado salad: 333 kcal per serving
Figs with prosciutto and goat's cheese: 190 kcal per serving
Fish and chips: 837 kcal per serving
Fish patties: 237 kcal per patty; 178 per slider; 71 per ball
Fish pie (with salmon): 693 kcal per serving (4 portions); 462 kcal per serving (6 portions)
Flapjacks: 305 kcal per flapjack
French onion soup: 431 kcal per serving
Fruit leather: 55 kcal per serving (4 portions)
Fruit tea bread: 2,018 kcal for whole cake (168 kcal per slice, if cut into 12 slices)

Glazed chicken wings: 540 kcal per serving (4 portions); 360 kcal per serving (6 portions)
Glazed oranges with almonds: 392 kcal per serving
Green beans with almonds and lemon zest: 100 kcal per serving
Greens with bacon and garlic: 95 kcal per serving
Guacamole: 176 kcal per serving (4 portions)

Halloumi, watercress and pomegranate salad: 350 kcal per serving

Ham and split pea soup: 474 kcal per serving (4 portions); 316 kcal per serving (6 portions)

Ham hock with vegetables: 500 kcal per serving

Hash browns: 208 kcal per serving

Herby brown rice: 300 kcal per serving

Home-made baked beans: 273 kcal per serving

Home-made granola: 391 kcal per serving (with 200ml whole milk)

Honey and vanilla panna cotta: 447 kcal per serving

Hummus: 117 kcal per serving (4 portions)

Kedgeree: 381 kcal per serving

Lentil and spinach soup: 278 kcal per serving (4 portions); 185 kcal per serving (6 portions)

Lime and ginger cheesecake: 544 kcal per serving

Mango lassi ice lollies: 40 kcal per lolly

Maple and pecan tarts: 712 kcal per tart

Mediterranean frittata: 220 kcal per serving

Multigrain seeded bread: 2,140 kcal for whole loaf (107 kcal per slice, if cut into 20 slices)

Pea, asparagus and broad bean frittata: 252 kcal per serving

Pea purée: 125 kcal per serving

Peach and almond crumble: 366 kcal per serving (4 portions); 244 kcal per serving (6 portions)

Peaches and cream ice lollies: 104 kcal per lolly

Pea, pesto and spelt salad: 431 kcal per serving

Pitta pizzas: about 450 kcal per pizza (depending on toppings)

Pitted bagels with avocado, tomato and bacon: 211 kcal per half bagel

Pitted bagels with cream cheese and smoked salmon: 279 kcal per half bagel

Pitted bagels with egg mayonnaise: 200 kcal per half bagel

Plum compote: 154 kcal per serving (4 portions)

Poached eggs with avocado on toast: 398 kcal per serving (1 egg)

Pork, bean and sweet potato chilli: 413 kcal per serving

Potato, root vegetable and garlic mash: 145 kcal per serving

Potato salad: 266 kcal per serving

Pot-roast chicken: 393 kcal per serving

Power balls: 85 kcal per ball (20 balls)

Prawn cocktail in avocado boats: 274 kcal per serving

Proper porridge: 452 kcal per serving

Ragù sauce: 571 kcal per serving (4 portions); 381 kcal per serving (6 portions)

Rainbow salad: 270 kcal per serving

Red slaw: 183 kcal per serving

Risotto with spring vegetables: 407 kcal per serving

Roast beetroot dip: 86 kcal per serving (4 portions)

Roast potatoes: 300 kcal per serving

Roast root vegetables (with honey): 179 kcal per serving

Roast root vegetables (without honey): 164 kcal per serving

Roast tomato pasta: 405 kcal per serving

Roast tomato soup with mozzarella balls: 250 kcal per serving

Roast vegetable and couscous salad: 283 kcal per serving

Salmon niçoise: 400 kcal per serving

Salmon tartare: 195 kcal per serving

Salmon with lentils: 494 kcal per serving

Sea bass with mushrooms and potatoes: 342 kcal per serving

Shepherd's pie: 660 kcal per serving

Slow-roast Moroccan lamb: 280 kcal per serving (4 portions); 185 kcal per serving (6 portions)

Smashed new potatoes: 271 kcal per serving

Strawberry and blueberry ice lollies: 30 kcal per lolly

Sweet potato fries: 223 kcal per serving

Vegetable crisps: 100 kcal per serving (4 servings)

Victoria sponge cake: 4,125 kcal for whole cake (344 kcal per slice, if cut into 12 slices)

Warm quinoa salad with avocado and broad beans: 180 kcal per serving

Yoghurt-marinated chicken: 212 kcal per serving

Index

Thank you all

Thanks to all the gang at Orion, especially Loulou Clark and Helen Ewing . . . thank you for being so enthusiastic! I've loved every moment. And special thanks to Amanda Harris who had me at 'sugar-free choc mousse'. Who'd have thought it was even possible to make sugar-free taste this good? Thank you for your support and guidance, and thank you for loving Kate Bush as much as I do!

Andrew Hayes-Watkins for the photos. What can I say Andrew? Our shoot days were such a gas!!! Thank you for being so lovely.

Paul Palmer-Edwards for the design. The book looks amazing. Thank you.

Catherine Phipps for recipes. OMG Catherine . . . you rock. You have taught me so much. I CAN POACH AN EGGGGGGGGGGGG!!! Thanks for also rising to the banoffee pie challenge. You nailed it.

Food stylists Anna Burges-Lumsden and Kate Blinman for making the food look so yum.

Jinny Johnson for helping with the words. I have loved comparing cooking notes with you. I love your company and you have such a nice energy to you I just want to be around you lots . . . thank you for 'getting' me.

Rowan for telling me that I can write a book and it doesn't have to be about me! And to Emily and George, the best agents ever. You keep me sane!

To AJ, Michael Douglas and Cheryl Phelps-Gardiner . . . without you I would look like a bag lady!

And to my delicious husband and beautiful children for being my guinea pigs and expert tasters!